AF394422

THE VILLAGE
ON THE EDGE OF
THE WORLD

Also by Herta Müller from Granta Books

FICTION

The Land of Green Plums
The Appointment
The Hunger Angel
The Fox was Ever the Hunter

NON-FICTION

Cristina and Her Double: Selected Essays

THE VILLAGE ON THE EDGE OF THE WORLD

Writing and Surviving Ceaușescu's Romania

Herta Müller

in conversation with Angelika Klammer

Translated from the German by Kate McNaughton

GRANTA

Granta Publications, 12 Addison Avenue, London W11 4QR

First published in Great Britain by Granta Books, 2026

Copyright © 2014 by Carl Hanser Verlag GmbH & Co. KG, München
English translation copyright © Kate McNaughton 2026

Originally published in Germany in 2014 under the title
Mein Vaterland war ein Apfelkern by Carl Hanser Verlag, Munich

The list of Herta Müller's previous works referred to in this book,
on pages 247–8, constitutes an extension of this copyright page.

A CIP catalogue record for this book is available from the British Library.

1 3 5 7 9 8 6 4 2

ISBN 978 1 78378 817 0 (hardback)
ISBN 978 1 78378 819 4 (ebook)

Typeset in Garamond by Patty Rennie

Printed and bound by CPI Group (UK) Ltd, Croydon, CR0 4YY

www.granta.com

The manufacturer's authorised representative in the EU for product safety is
BGC Sustainability & Compliance, 7 avenue du Général Leclerc,
75014 Paris, France (gpsr@baldwinglobalconsulting.com)

Contents

'The arc that stretches from a child herding cows in the valley to the Stockholm City Hall is a strange one. Here, too, as is so often the case, I am standing beside myself.'
Herta Müller, in her acceptance speech
for the Nobel Prize in Literature

In this book, Herta Müller charts this arc once more, in discussion with her editor, Angelika Klammer. The conversations that led to this book took place in Berlin in December 2013 and January 2014. To them have been added, in a revised form, central passages regarding *The Hunger Angel*, taken from a conversation that took place in Berlin in August 2009 and which was published under the title 'Wie lange bleibt man eitel?' ['How long does one stay vain?'] in the literary journal *Volltext. Zeitschrift für Literatur* 4/2009.

Owls on the Roof

'The landscape of childhood,' you write in one of your essays, 'defines how we view landscapes for the rest of our years. The landscape of our childhood socialises us surreptitiously. It creeps into us.' In your childhood, cornfields ran round the entire world.

Those huge Socialist cornfields. When you stood in the middle of one, surrounded by the dense cornstalks, the field was a forest. It towered above you, and you couldn't see out of it. But it was missing the canopy above: there was no shade, the sun would blaze down on your head all day long, all summer long. And then, in late autumn, there were the countless forgotten fields. They were left barren and unkempt, they weren't harvested. You could see them from afar. The snow would come and they would appear to roam across the plain. And so, seen from afar, from outside, the fields were like herds, roaming upright around the whole world. Upright, yes.

In this oversized landscape, the child feels lost; she experiences her first great loneliness.

Things have stayed that way too. I believe there are two kinds of people, and what differentiates them is how they experience landscapes. Some people like to climb a mountain, stand with their feet almost touching the clouds and command the valley with their mind, with their gaze. They breathe freely up there, take great gulps of air and feel their chests expand. As for the others, when they stand up there and look down – that's when they truly feel lost. I belong to the lost ones: my throat chokes up. The wider the view, the more constricted and harried I feel, as if I might be about to keel over and die. My very existence is called into question. I think this happens because of the endlessness I project myself into, in the face of which I am essentially nothing. I look out at a vast landscape and I feel a great sense of hopelessness.

I used to experience Nature as physical harassment. It is pitiless, after all: it freezes, it burns, and you burn or freeze with it. The searing hot summers, the thirst in your throat, the dust of the earth: you have no defences against any of it. Your body is not made for these conditions – you ache and grow weary. You are not, in fact, a stone or a tree; the stuff you are made of cannot withstand Nature. You are laughable, transient. Whenever I worked in the fields, I would be filled with grief. I did not want to feel this grief: it only made my efforts even more laborious. But every time I set to work, the feeling would come, and it was always against me. It would not leave me in peace. It was a baseless, stupid grief, and each time it was as if it had been there waiting for me, in the field or in the river valley. How long will this body belong to you, it asked. How long will you be alive? You can stand in this landscape as often as you like, you don't belong here. I found Nature hostile. In winter, too. Then, later on, I learnt that natural phenomena are used to torture people in prisons, in camps. The Arctic Circle and the desert, the frost and heat: they can kill and so can be used as instruments of torture, to destroy people. This thought kept occurring to me. Later, when I lived in the city, I still couldn't understand how other people could feel exalted in Nature. They stand on a mountain and look down at the valley with their eyes and toes and are happy. How do they do it?

So Nature seems hostile because we are at its mercy, and must assert ourselves in the face of it? In your texts, Nature is never presented as a place of play or contemplation – all it has to offer is hard work.

For people in the village, the landscape was neither ugly nor beautiful: it was a place of work, a usable surface. Farmers need the landscape in order to survive, and the weather decides whether or not anything will come of that year's crop. And then there is Nature's incessant protests: sometimes it will flood everything, or make everything wither; sometimes you'll have hail or a storm and the whole harvest is destroyed. I never liked the countryside. And yet I had a very close relationship with plants. Observing the landscape helped me feel less alone. I had to be down in the valley all day long – an endless stretch of time. So what could I do? Well, I busied myself with the plants. It just happened. I wasn't doing it consciously, but I was looking for something to hold on to.

I tasted them all. I ate a bit of a different plant each day. They tasted tart, sour, tangy or bitter. Clearly, I never happened on anything poisonous. Perhaps my long, daily loneliness gave me a kind of instinct for what was safe, like an animal. Why, for example, did I never eat a deadly nightshade or a lily of the valley? The valley lay on the edge of a forest, there were plenty of lilies of the valley.

You describe how these actions express a desire to resemble the plants over time – perhaps even to undergo a metamorphosis – since the plants can cope with this landscape, while the child cannot.

I always thought the plants were at home in the valley; they were happy with themselves and with the world, while I could only lumber around. I didn't know what to do with myself. And I thought that if I ate enough of the plants, then maybe I too would belong, because the body I was walking around in would assimilate with them. I hoped that the plants I had eaten would change my skin, my flesh, in such a way that I would better fit in in the valley. It was an attempt to make myself close to the plants, to metamorphose. Metamorphose – the word wouldn't have occurred to me, I wouldn't even have known it. I knew only this desire to find a place for myself, to preserve myself, to make time bearable. You see your whole finitude, which you don't have a word for either – but one doesn't only worry about the things one has words for. I didn't need to name an experience to learn how to cope with it, or at least not using abstract terms. And even if I had needed those words, it was good that I didn't know them. There are some feelings, especially in childhood, that are as concrete as the body itself – no more and no less. They are simply there, and that is enough. It's more than enough. For me, it was being foreign: I was constantly alone with these plants and yet I still didn't belong. I remained foreign and it was diffi-cult to bear. They were growing tired of me, and one day, probably soon, the Earth would gobble me up.

> *The field only feeds people so that it can gobble them*
> *up at a later point. You view this cycle as aggressive,*
> *not gentle or natural, and one in which human*
> *beings are nothing more than 'candidate[s] for*
> *the waxworks of death'.*

People plant something, it grows, then they harvest it and eat it. I thought: in your life you eat the flour from, say, thirty bags of grain, or fifty or a hundred, the wheat feeds you until the earth gobbles you up. For me, death has always meant that the earth devours you. And I thought the Earth was so large because so many people and animals had already died.

I always tried to find the right way to measure things. If I eat my bodyweight in clover, then the clover will like me, I thought. But I didn't know if it would be a good or a bad thing for it to like me. Or if I ate a whole patch of ribwort, as big as a bed, then perhaps I would be able to sleep for a while, just like the cows laying lazily in the grass. I also believed that each breath you take is counted. That they are threaded like glass beads on to a piece of string, to form a chain, and that once this breath chain reaches a length that stretches from your mouth to the graveyard, then you die. Because each breath is invisible, nobody knows the length of their breath chain. So nobody knows when they or any-one else will die. Similarly, I thought that if you were to cut off all the hair a man grows over the course of his life and stuff it into a sack, then he would die once this sack was as heavy as him. The question was always how long someone would live. I wanted to pin a measure on Time, so that it would become an object that you could see, that you could handle. But I never knew what the right unit of measurement was, so not only was I wrestling with this enigma of Time and its alternating languor and agitation, but I was also thinking up all of these absurd, fruitless calculations, which left me even more scared.

And because I wanted to resemble the plants, I talked aloud to them. And I would spend hours laying down various flowers next to each other, comparing their faces, and pairing them up and marrying them to each other.

Your task while working in the valley was to look after the cows. As animals, they occupy an intermediate position: they do not belong to the landscape as intimately as plants do, they are not rooted in it, but they are closer to it than human beings are.

I was convinced that plants are only motionless during the day – that at night, when everyone is asleep, they walk around like animals and visit each other, or simply go and take a look at a different part of the world. That their roots stay in the earth and wait for them, and that towards morning, when it gets light, they return to them, and that that is why they appear to grow in the same place.

Each day, I would also observe – unthinkingly at times, and sometimes with interest – these cows who were sufficient unto themselves. As soon as they reached the field, they would bend down and feed until they were herded home in the evening. They didn't need anything else; they didn't gaze at the sky. They barely looked at me either, thank

God. They would swing their heads, because the meddlesome flies were crawling into their eyes. The only beautiful thing about them was their big eyes. They shone like water in a deep well and reflected me as if I were growing crooked out of the earth. Sometimes I felt sorry for those sad eyes – or perhaps I was feeling sorry for myself. There were also days when the cows would run around the meadow instead of feeding. And I would run after them, because I had to make sure they didn't run on to the State-owned fields. If they did, we would have to pay the fines for any damage they did there. Chasing after them was unbearable. It left me tired to death, and filled with hatred for those cows.

How many cows were you looking after, then?

Most of the time we had three cows; now and then we would also have two or three calves. But once the calves were the requisite weight, we had to hand them over to the State. Three cows may not sound like a lot, but each cow was a huge thing and not as good-natured as it looked. Each one was wild and strong as a tractor, very stubborn and irascible. On those wild days I grew desperate. I learnt how to cry while running and how to run while crying.

The trains that passed by were the only things that gave your days any structure. In them sat city folk in beautiful summer dresses. The child gets as close as possible to the tracks, sees jewellery gleam, another life flash by – and waves.

Yes, the valley was quiet, you could hear the trains from far off and so I could get close to the tracks in good time.

The train was like a visitation. As if guests had come to the valley, people of a type that never usually came to the village. As soon as the train hissed in the distance, I would already be untying my apron, so that I could use it to wave. In the morning, as I was getting dressed, I would consider which apron to choose – I'd wear the plain blue apron if I'd worn the flowery or spotted one the day before. I wanted to wave with a different apron, just in case the same passengers were on board each day. Unfortunately, the train was very short, just two or three carriages, no more, and once they had passed I felt abandoned, as if a terrible big white door had slammed shut right in front of my nose. I would walk away from the tracks slowly and put my apron back on as I walked. The train was always full of city folk, or well-dressed village folk returning from the city. When village folk went to the city, they would put on their Sunday best, so that their ugliness was less conspicuous. I had been to the city a few times with my mother, to go to the doctor or buy shoes. People in the city didn't get so dirty; they didn't spend the whole day in the sun, or in the dust of the cornfields; they remained on the pavements, in the shade of big buildings. Even early in the morning, the men would already be wearing short-sleeved shirts, and the women had high-heeled shoes and patent-leather handbags. In the passing train, too, I would see them, standing in the middle of the aisle at the open window: they were made-up, wearing brooches, necklaces, their fingernails painted red. And I – in my misery, my filth and loneliness – would wave at them with my old red or blue apron. If I had been born elsewhere or had different parents, I would muse every now and again, would I now be a different child? Or would I be the same child, regardless of who my parents were and where I was born? Would I always remain the same child, fused to my skin, regardless of what I wanted to be and how many plants I ate? Does everyone remain fused to themselves? I always felt that these thoughts were forbidden, that nobody should find out that I was grappling with such things. Nor should anybody see that I ate and married flowers. It would have been awful if anyone had caught me, because they'd have thought I wasn't normal.

But you didn't get caught. Was it your family's
taciturnity – working or sitting next to each other
in silence – that protected you?

No, I never got caught. No one could tell what I was thinking – they couldn't tell anything about me. You couldn't tell anything about anybody. When night fell outside, everyone would come to the dining table for supper. We would eat, and no one asked anyone else how their day had been. Secrets clung to each of us. I was convinced that everyone was sad from their forehead to their toes, that everyone had these claws piercing their hearts and that we were all fighting against them. But they never betrayed their struggle: they kept it hidden inside them. I thought this village grief had everyone in its grip, that it was evenly spread across everything. You couldn't escape it.

Because one can't escape it, you write, one must
'endure grief and learn to understand it'. And right
afterwards: 'Childhood is probably the most confused
part of life. So much more is built up and torn down
at once than will ever be again later.'

I was very often sad as a child, because I was alone too much, and because I had to do a lot of work around the house too – cleaning the windows, for example. There were maybe a hundred windowpanes, triple sets of double casement windows. By the time you had finished washing them, you'd lost the entire day. Well, all right, you could do a bit of a slapdash job, but it still ate up a lot of time. I was raised to clean windows for the rest of my life. I haven't cleaned windows since, but I know obedience to a nauseating extreme. You're supposed to be prepared for something, you're supposed to view it as absolutely necessary in life. But in your head the opposite thought appears, you say to yourself: no more window-cleaning, ever again. You free yourself. This internal, personal freedom, at least, is easy to achieve.

Your mother's life was entirely absorbed in these tasks.
She would clean and sweep, she had a lot of brooms:
a kitchen broom, a cow barn broom, a pig-pen
broom and a hen-house broom, a woodshed broom,
a smokehouse broom and two street brooms, one for
the pavement and the other for the grass.

It's an exaggeration of course, but I used the repetition of the word 'broom' as a literary device to portray her cleaning mania. This cleaning addiction was probably not equally pronounced in every household, but for my mother it was her true purpose in life. When she wasn't out in the fields, she was cleaning the house. She is one of those people who can't simply sit and think, they always need their body to be active too. Her cleaning was pure habit – it had nothing to do with dirt any more. And just as I am averse to doing physical work, these people had an opposing internal drive: to exert their bodies. They were hell-bent on working, they strove to completely wear themselves out. In the case of my mother, it may also have had something to do with the five years she spent in a labour camp.* Drudgery was a means of retaining order, of keeping a hold on life, a way of holding one's feelings at arm's length. As for people like us, we set our minds to work in order to escape how we are feeling. But we are no different to my mother; we simply put up different defences. For my mother, working was her natural disposition. It was mechanical, she didn't get tired; she was both entirely absent and completely present while doing it. She became whatever she was doing with her hands. She disappeared as a person and became an engine, a process in an apron and a dress. This is how I explain to myself why she never grew tired, why she never slowed down. Her hands were always working, except when she slept. I have no idea what she thought about while she worked. Perhaps she'd learnt to think of nothing in the labour camp? Is it a piece of good fortune to forget your head and selflessly open yourself up to the most arduous work? Who knows.

---

* Around 70,000 Romanian Germans were deported into forced labour by the Soviets at the end of the Second World War, mainly to camps in the Ukraine Soviet Socialist Republic. This was part of a wider policy of deporting ethnic Germans living throughout the European USSR during and after the war, first out of fear that they might collaborate with the Nazi invaders, and then as a form of war reparations for the damage inflicted by the Nazi regime on the Soviet Union.

*Silence at the dining table, being so absorbed in
one's work that one becomes pure process – this creates
an atmosphere in which a sense of belonging together
is primarily manufactured through shared habits
and cooking pots.*

That is the view of an adult. For me, as a child, it was simply how things were – whether I felt good about it or not is a different question. People whose bodies are at work all day don't talk about themselves. All that is talked about is what they've done: the movements of their working hands. But if somebody never says a word about themselves, how can you develop a sense of belonging together? Perhaps the fact of belonging together was so strong that we didn't need to actually feel connected to each other. Everybody viewed it as normal that we belonged together, but this was not expressed in words or gestures. After all, when you sit at a table together, when you use the same door, the same cutlery and the same cooking pot, when your clothes hang next to each other on the washing line, there is something clear and valid about it: you belong together, these shared items and routines guarantee it. I don't know whether the others ever felt lonely, whether they ever wished that we engaged with each other more. I really don't think so though, and I certainly didn't expect anyone to poke around in my village grief back then. Talking about yourself – I only discovered that later, in the city.

When you write down your childhood, it becomes worse than it was. There is a sleight of hand at play in the child's perspective in literature. There is admittedly a lot that is real in there, but it's all conveyed through words arranged in sequence – words placed before, behind and after one another – whereas when you were living through it, everything was mixed up: one experience on top of the other, simultaneous and piled up.

As a child I wished that I didn't have to work so much, that I didn't always have to go into the valley, that I could play more, that maybe I could even spend more time with other children, but there was no cogent overarching aim to these desires, no ambition to realise them. They were subliminal. The black-and-white of words on the page is a different imaginative realm to the thoughts of childhood. It is an artificially replicated world of words, reconstructed thirty years after the fact.

Is this also why the child in Nadirs *has no allies, or friends at school, no person they trust? In all your other books there is somebody with whom the first-person narrator shares her experiences, whether happy or unhappy.*

Perhaps I turned away from potential allies because I knew that what was inside my head was forbidden, because I didn't believe myself to be capable of being normal. Because I did in fact know that it wasn't normal to think that plants walked around at night, that life threads our breaths on to a chain and measures them, that the Earth gobbles us up. It was surreal. But religion is just as surreal, that added to it all: God is everywhere; He sees everything; the dead go to Heaven. I would search for dead neighbours or dead animals in the shape of the clouds and I would find them there, too. I knew that I would run into problems with God. If He saw everything, then He also knew what I was thinking in my head. OK, he wasn't doing anything about it yet, but at some point he would punish me.

The fundamental problem was that these thoughts and actions didn't fit within the framework of what was permissible – so how was I supposed to tell anyone about them? I assumed that everyone felt the same as I did, that they were all stuffed full of secrets, of this grief that they couldn't do anything about, which the village produced in people's heads. Everyone had these claws piercing their hearts, but they kept it to themselves. This was how it had to be; everyone had to keep everything to themselves.

Very rarely, people would slip up. When once, on the way home after Mass, I said to my grandmother that the Virgin Mary's heart was a watermelon sliced in half, she answered: that may be, but you must never say this to anybody. And thus the topic was closed. In response to such slip-ups, my grandmother would also sometimes say: don't think where you shouldn't. *Where*, she said, as if when thinking one went to an actual place – down an overly long street or into an unfamiliar room.

She talked about thinking as if it had feet. She was shy, monosyllabic. She spoke less than anyone else. And when she did say something, it was always short and flat, in a very dry tone. But her words would flutter inside me. They would churn me up and follow me for a long time. And they would keep reoccurring to me. Now I know that such sentences were more closely related to silence than to speaking – perhaps they were not even spoken at all, just thought out loud. The length of the sentence kept getting shorter as it was spoken. This speaking without wanting to, cryptic as it is, imprints itself word for word on your memory without you asking it to. I think these are innocent aphorisms – they don't need any intention, they don't even need themselves.

God strikes the girl as a judging, punishing authority. Mary, in contrast, is a radiant Queen of Heaven; the girl kept paying her visits, brought her small offerings such as sweets, a match, a hair clasp.

She was so pretty, a huge plaster doll with her heart painted on to the outside of her light-blue dress. She wasn't a sculpture as far as I was concerned, she was *the* Mary, the one from Heaven. I never asked myself why she was here in the church and not up in Heaven. It was a normal place for her to show herself; she stood there and I was with her. Her long, sky-blue dress, who in the village had anything like that? And the fact that I made her various offerings, that wasn't allowed either, no one should find out about that. It wasn't straightforward, but the world wasn't straightforward. I had considerable problems shuffling all of this around in my mind and coming to terms with it. It may be that I wanted to ingratiate myself with her so that she would tell the Lord that He shouldn't punish me too harshly. Once you'd confessed, you had to say the sentence: I will earnestly improve myself and shun the opportunity to sin. As if I had sought out sin . . . Sin had sought *me* out! I knew after every confession that I would never be able to keep this promise, that I had lied. And thus every confession ended with a fresh lie. And that wasn't going to stay hidden from the Lord, was it?

Religion fosters fear, surveillance and control on the one hand – you had cowslip, or key of heaven, hanging

*in your house, that also saw everything – but on the
other, it provides material for images. God, who, with
His long, white beard, perches up in the trees above.
And the dead are driven as clouds across the heavens,
like army recruits.*

Religion was never any comfort – all it ever did was threaten you and apportion guilt.

Children think both surreally and very concretely. But the surreal is of course concrete. I was only applying what the grown-ups said to me: God is everywhere; all the dead are in Heaven. So I searched for them and saw faces in the clouds, which then also looked like someone I knew. When the clouds were driven along by the wind, it was clear to me that God was pushing the dead around, like an army. He knows what they've done, and so who knows how He'll push me around. For the time being He's still watching me, but the evidence against me is mounting up.

*Fear – in particular, intangible fear – is also strongly
connected to the night: it creeps right up to the houses,
leans its back against the fences and everything goes
pitch-black and dead silent.*

Darkness is eerie, because it encloses you and you drown in it – your surroundings disappear, you can't see yourself. Night is an uncertain time. In sleep, you are taken away from yourself. But we're lucky that in sleep we don't feel the uncertainty of the night. When you wake up, it's over: you are yourself again, you're like new. And if you don't wake up, you're dead. I was always afraid in the dark:

the air was black ink or black wool, thick mud or a huge animal pelt. Darkness shows you what death will look like when it comes. For death was always in the village; after all, it was simply the other, later stage of life. And just like life, it had its ways, its strategies and aims. It knew all of us, and had different plans for every person in the village. My fear of the night also had a lot to do with glass. At night, everything became fragile, as though made out of black glass. The night-time trees, the wind in the gutters, the rain, the cold, the whetted stars and the frosted-glass moon. And I would twitch my eyes in the dark until the stars wobbled, along with the outlines of the buildings and fences. I was convinced that objects, just like plants, walked here and there during the night and didn't return to their original places until it began to get light – always at the last moment, just before they got caught. I would quickly flick on the light on the veranda, to catch the tables and chairs making their final moves. But I never succeeded, I was always a fraction of a second too late. The furniture was clever, particularly the mirrors: they knew what was going on inside people. They could see into you. People said the Devil sits in the mirror. When someone died, you had to cover all the mirrors in your house, so that they wouldn't take the dead person's soul. At night, I was also afraid of the very tall man who lived at the end of the village. People said he didn't need to work; he got money from the city every month because he had sold his skeleton to the museum. The word 'skeleton' was creepy, I'd never heard it other than in connection with this man. Through this word, 'skeleton', the tall man seemed like the wooden frame of trees or long ladders. In my mind, he was more closely related to wood than to us people, and wood did not need to sleep, so he would walk around at night, just like all things made of wood did.

The fact of having to cover the mirror, so that the Devil would not steal the soul of the dead person, is one of the types of superstition that you describe as poetic.

There was also the superstition with the owls: that when they pick out a particular roof and hoot there, someone in the house will die. There were many roofs and many owls. You would listen out for whether the hooting was far away or nearby.

Superstition, be it the Devil in the mirror or the owls on the roof, is poignant. There is something magical about it, it is basically poetry – the poetry of people who do not write. These are connections that transcend themselves and are dauntingly beautiful, linguistically and figuratively, when I look back on them today. But when you *practise* superstition, there is nothing poetic about it any more – then it is a reality just like any other. If the door creaks, I have to oil its hinges, and if someone dies, I have to cover the mirror, so that their soul won't go off with the Devil but will find its way to Heaven. In both these cases, there is a remedy that takes the form of practical action. But there is still a big difference between the two: the door stops creaking once it has been oiled, but even once you have covered the mirror, your fear of the Devil does not go away. You do what superstition commands, but you do not know whether you did so in time or for long enough – you cannot rely on superstition as you can on a hinge. You do what you're told, but the uncertainty remains, because it has a poetic dimension, which cannot be controlled.

*Fear, superstition and loneliness shape the world
of the village. In contrast, affection or tenderness are
only expressed covertly – if at all. You have to sniff
them out. For example, in the question: 'Do you
have a handkerchief?'*

The question about the handkerchief showed me that my mother worried about me a little. Or that she worried about my external appearance at least. As a child from a respectable home, you had to carry a clean, neatly ironed handkerchief, just in case: to blow your nose, cry into, wipe your hands on, to dress your wounds, to fashion a handle out of it which you could use to carry things, or to make a purse, or a head covering against the sun and rain. I also kept finding lost handkerchiefs, and I lost a few myself. The most precious handkerchiefs were unique pieces: embroidered by hand, or with monograms or crocheted edges. Handkerchiefs are some of the most protean things in the world. Once, I saw someone drop down dead in the middle of the city, and watched as a passer-by covered the dead man's face with his newspaper. Another passer-by then removed the newspaper, crumpled it up, stuffed it wordlessly into his briefcase, and covered the face with his handkerchief instead. The first man said: well, I don't have a handkerchief on me right now. Half the page of the newspaper had been a picture of Ceaușescu – as it was every day. But I don't think that was the reason for replacing the newspaper with a handkerchief, or at least not the only one. Even without a picture of the dictator, the newspaper was not suitable as a first, ambulatory death shroud. It made this sudden death on an asphalted park path even more miserable. The handkerchief, however, changed the picture:

it nestled and protected, it was not just a practical gesture, it contained tenderness, a wordless condolence. I forgot to walk on; I was churned up inside and lame on the outside, as one is in such moments. Filled with curiosity and disgust, you stop as if glued to the spot, for much longer than you wanted to. The two passers-by were long gone. I grew sentimental in the belief that perhaps sympathy was burgeoning inside people again, in spite of all the brutality of this broken Socialism – that perhaps empathy can appear as suddenly as falseness and denunciation. I cried, but the dead man was not the cause, only the occasion. Faced with this public death on the asphalt, I wept for the whole picture, which struck me diffusely – the loathsome dissembling, the constant menace and the wild fear that governed the State – and above all for myself.

When I look back at my childhood, it wasn't just our feeling of belonging together that went unseen: the same applied to all our feelings. If you never speak a word about yourself, you never betray any feelings at all. I think I would have been alarmed if my mother had suddenly cuddled me. I wouldn't even have perceived it as cuddling, I wouldn't have been able to adjust to it, I wouldn't have interpreted it as tenderness – I wouldn't have been able to bear it at all in that unexpected moment. I think one can be just as alarmed by unexpected tenderness as by unexpected violence. If you are regularly beaten as a child, you lose any horror associated with it. You feel the pain, that doesn't change. But you lose the horror. Something peculiar happens, and this is the worst thing about it: your sense of dignity is upturned. How can I put it? Regular beatings do not make you physically insensitive, but you develop a kind of desire, in defiance of your own understanding, to feel your own body in pain, to become the version of you engendered by that pain – because this feeling is so different to when you are not in pain. The violence gives rise to a sweetness that is reprehensible according to your own moral standards. And you even have to disavow this sweetness in your own eyes so that you can desire it again the next time. And it gets even more complicated still: in this sweetness which you are disavowing because it is unacceptable, you sense dignity. The dignity of the body, perhaps, before which your mind is ashamed. After all, when dignity is created *while* and *because* you are being humiliated, then you really are seriously damaged. I was given a beating every day for everything and nothing: for a stain on my Sunday best, a bad mark at school, a poorly cleaned windowpane, for returning home with the cows too early or too late. Sometimes the beatings were administered by hand, sometimes using a tea towel, a wooden spoon or a broom. It wasn't like this for everybody, but it was for a lot of children. Clips round the ear and light beatings weren't even worth mentioning, they were part and parcel of everyday life. In her rage, my mother would scream that she regretted every blow that didn't hit its mark. For her it was about hitting her mark, the reasons for the beatings were secondary – you could always find a reason. And I was so numb to it that I didn't make any effort to behave in such a way as to not be punished. I knew I would get a beating regardless, the beating had more to do with her than with me anyway. Now I know that she was hardened and broken: she had only just survived her five years in a Russian labour camp, and they were not yet far behind her when I was born. So many people around her had starved or frozen to death; she had been luckier than them, but she returned destitute, married quickly, had a child which went blue and died after it was born, and a second one shortly afterwards – which was me. She did not speak about the camp, and if she did she always used the same, cryptic sentences in which she herself never appeared. She would say: wind is colder than snow, thirst is a worse torment than hunger. She forced her life into a merciless normality and this included, for her part, the beatings, and for my part the numbing and the exchange of dignity for humiliation.

You came across a more extreme form of this dynamic later on, in a nursery.

Over twenty years later, I was a nursery teacher for a few weeks. The headteacher briefed me on my first day that we were to sing the national anthem first thing every morning. Then she showed me the canes on a rack: long and short, thick and thin. The children were primed for beatings. When I got close to a child, they would press their eyes closed, turn their face away from me and say: don't hit me. But the other children would shout in a chorus: go on, give it to him, give it to him. It made my skin crawl, and I would think of my younger self; I knew how they were feeling, these children who had been trained to be beaten. I never touched the canes, but the children were already brutalised and hysterical. They despised me because I didn't beat them – they *asked* me to beat them, as if it were a gift, a mercy. They did not react to words, not even if I screamed. My attempts to assert myself all failed. Working in the nursery, I came to understand my former self. I knew what it meant to ask for a beating, for the humiliation to be trumped by an impertinent inner pride – I knew all that from my mother. The fact that the nursery, and therefore the State, viewed the education of children as synonymous with beating them was even more egregious than bellowing out the national anthem every morning. But I think it all went hand in hand: without this idea of humanity being made out of concrete and this ideology that crushed everything, there would not have been any canes in the nursery.

But what remains incomprehensible to me to this day are my fits of laughter. I often felt compelled to laugh at the most inappropriate moments: when something valuable dropped to the floor and shattered, when someone fell and hurt themselves. The worst was at funerals: I would look at the rosaries between people's fingers, the yellow-grey tongue of the singing cantor, the priest's toecaps like black snouts under his white lace cowl – and my mouth would slip into laughter. It was my attention to these details, stripped of their wider context, that did it. I couldn't avoid the laughing fits, and then, once they'd started, I couldn't stop them. I wasn't feeling joyful at all, nor was I making fun of anything. I couldn't connect any image I saw to its wider context, to what it really was, at that point. I was probably dividing up what I could not bear as a whole. And as such, in laughing, my sympathy was greater than if I had been crying. I was distraught, but nobody seemed to understand this. I didn't understand it myself, and I didn't try to justify the laughing fits. To do that I would have had to explain them, and even now I still have no explanation. I would endure a wordless beating for every one of them, and I was ashamed of myself and knew that I deserved it. There's something I still don't know to this day, though: is there a form of laughter that is more profoundly sad than weeping? A laughter that has fallen on its head, tumbled upside-down into an abyss? At any rate, a laughing fit is harsh and cutting, it hurts inside, it is an attack, an extravagance, an outbreak of all sorts of things – but it is no outbreak of joy.

The laughing fits allowed me to offload the village grief I carried around with me, which was continuously produced, both individually and collectively, by all the props and tools of the village. Every funeral would stay with me for an eternity, and I couldn't eat meat for days afterwards. I have never tried to explain this illogical connection to myself. Even if I were to consult a psychological expert, the most they would be able to offer are interpretations – there is no certainty in the accursed connections between the internal and the external.

The Rhyme Knows the Score

*You connect the hardness within your family, the
blows, the numbing, to what you call 'damage'
from the camps and the war.*

They had all been damaged in some way. The village was so
isolated, so far away from the world. It stood there like a box
in the landscape, with no asphalt road, just this train that
briefly whooshed past. And everyone was born in the village, married in the village, had children in the village and
worked in the fields around the village. You lived, sowed,
harvested and ate from those fields, until the Earth gobbled
you up. You did everything on the same patch of land,
no one ever strayed from it – everything was always the
same, for over three hundred years. But then these clueless
peasants were dragged off into the world. My grandfather
into the First World War, my father into the Second, while
my mother was deported to a Soviet labour camp. War
and deportation forced them to leave the village. Even the
animals were drafted into the army: my grandfather had
handwritten and stamped death certificates for his horses
that had fallen in the First World War. That was something I couldn't understand as a child: that there were death

certificates for horses, but not for the people who didn't return from the war. After the Second World War, many people simply remained lost forever. They were classified as missing, because there was neither any sign of them being alive nor news that they were dead.

Veronika, who also lived in the village, was the same age as my mother. Her husband was one of those who had gone missing. Twenty years had passed since the war and she still said: when the wind rattles the alley gate at night, I think perhaps it is my husband after all. She knew that the wind wasn't her husband, she said, but, unlike his death, the wind and the alley gate were real. She remained alone in her long house with its many rooms, empty animal pens and barns for the rest of her life. She had five guinea fowl, speckled white like snow on grey silk, and a tree in her backyard that bore the earliest cherries in the village. She wasn't complaining about her life when she made the comment about the wind at the gate. She wouldn't have said it at all if I hadn't asked if she had a husband. She also didn't place any value on my understanding what she meant. If anything, she thought that I was still too young to imagine what waiting for somebody for twenty years was like. But in my own way, I did understand it: a gust of wind at the alley gate could very well be somebody coming home. It was perfectly normal, just like all the objects and plants walking around the village at night. Of course, I was ten years old at the time, and so I didn't know what twenty years of waiting meant for a woman – just that you could talk aloud to weeds and bushes and that you could even marry flowers to each other in the middle of the day. I always sought to attach a measure to time, so that it would become visible, but the measure 'twenty years' was one that eluded me.

And Veronika seemed ageless to me – perhaps because she lived in the house alone. I was too naive to understand her situation and the age difference between us. I would eat her cherries in early May and it never occurred to me as I did so that my entire life up until that point wasn't even half as long as the time she'd been waiting for her husband. I think it did her good that I didn't understand it, that I was so simple-minded. For me, there was no difference between me and her, save for her elegant guinea fowl. And uniting us was that never-spoken word: 'loneliness'. It wouldn't even have been possible to say the word, it didn't exist in our dialect. There was only the word 'alone', '*alleenig*', and we weren't alone when we were speaking to each other. But nevertheless, we recognised that we each had quite a lot to do with the word '*alleenig*'. Although I couldn't appreciate what twenty years meant, the word '*alleenig*' was visible on Veronika, it had grown round her mouth. Unlike on me, on her it was bright: she found purpose and strength in remaining steadfast. I think that, unlike me, Veronika lived in accordance with herself and what she was. She acknowledged the death of her husband, but still she waited for him, without him ever needing to come, as long as there was the alley gate and the wind.

Others did return, but could no longer find their way back to themselves. When, from one day to the next, someone who has never left these fifty square kilometres of land moves thousands of kilometres away in the world, it changes everything. My father went to war at the age of seventeen, with Hitler's SS. He survived, came back to the village and then never travelled beyond its surrounding area again. The furthest he ventured was to the city, thirty kilometres away. He was a lorry driver, and supplied the village shop with his *'rablament'*, as he put it – his old banger of a lorry. When he wanted to drive off, a second person had to be there to help start up the engine with the crank, before quickly throwing it into the trailer when the engine roared on and jumping into the cab. They'd then have to quickly hook the door closed using a piece of wire, because the handle had broken off. And in the bottom of the cab was a big hole; you could see the earth drive along with you. I was convinced that the lorry was standing still, that it was the road that was flowing beneath us.

The only time my mother left the village was for her deportation into forced labour. Women who, like my mother, had survived the camps were easy to distinguish, physically, from those who hadn't been deported, through their haircuts and clothing: those who had stayed at home, because they were too young or old during the time of deportations, the non-deported, in short, wore plaits and ankle-length pleated skirts, while the deported had short hair and short dresses. There was an unmistakable divide: the deportations were a watershed in the life of the village.

Short hair and dresses were a clear sign that life
had changed: it could no longer be connected to
what it was before.

In the camp, the women's heads were shaved for five years, sometimes as a punishment, sometimes because of the lice. And during their forced labour they wore the same rough Russian camp uniforms as the men. None of these women let their hair grow out again afterwards, or had ankle-length pleated skirts sewn for them – which says it all, really. The deportations put an end to three hundred years of peasant attire. It wasn't a conscious decision on the part of the villagers – it came of its own volition, from survival, from distress. It was a brutal consequence of the camps which was never spoken about. You can't escape the effects of five years of malnutrition, of water in your belly and legs. And there was something else the deported all had in common: instead of teeth they were left with rotten stumps, which had to be pulled out. They had to wear dentures in perpetuity, and they rattled around in their mouths, because when you are chronically malnourished your gums shrink away too. After her homecoming, the first thing my mother did, at the age of twenty-five, was to have two sets of dentures made by the dentist in our small town, one for the top set of teeth, one for the bottom. And all the others did too.

On top of the experience of war and the camps, which people in Eastern and Western Europe – whatever their differences – did share, came the fact that in Romania the year 1945 did not mark the end of fear, persecution, repression and terror.

Yes, in that post-war moment and in the following decades, democracies were created in Western Europe. But in Eastern Europe we had dictatorships. The Soviets installed their model of society: Stalinism. The military, police and secret services of all Eastern European nations were trained in Moscow, and Eastern Europe was full of Stalinist prisons and camps. Over the decades, the Russians kept making more graveyards in Eastern Europe. Nobody has ever tallied the dead in all these countries – they were probably equal to the number who died in the gulags of the Soviet

Union. Thousands were imprisoned, physically and psychologically crippled, or tortured to death for 'anti-Soviet agitation' through to the 1960s. And you weren't allowed to talk about any of this in Eastern Europe until 1989.

During the Second World War, Romania stood at Hitler's side almost until the end, with the fascist dictator Antonescu, but then it airbrushed its history, claiming to have been 'on the side of the victorious Soviet army'. As a fascist state, Romania also exterminated its Jewish population. Just as with the Nazis, there were racial laws, ghettos, pogroms; the Jews had to wear the Star of David, they were dispossessed. And the concentration camps in Transnistria were under Romanian management.

Stalinism then ensured that guilt was apportioned in a particularly malicious manner: the German minority was punished for these crimes, while the Romanians claimed to have been anti-fascists.

Under these circumstances, silence became the rule. Any statement about what you had experienced was dangerous, including anything private. And because the Romanians disavowed their crimes, my father denied the crimes of the SS to me – we had vicious arguments. As for my mother, she said nothing about the camp. My grandfather meanwhile was deemed by the State to belong to the 'exploitative class'. His fields, his colonial goods store, his gold bars, they were all expropriated. He had, however, sunk a few gold bars into the well in our courtyard – this was sometimes whispered about at the dining table on winter evenings. Years later, the well was pumped dry, because allegedly a cat had fallen into it. No cat had fallen in; my family simply wanted to check on the gold bars. But they were no longer to be found; they had seeped into the earth, disappeared without a trace. Perhaps they're now swimming at the centre of the Earth.

The village seemed almost counterfeit to me. It stood there as it always had, over the course of its dreary three hundred years, but in reality it had long been pulled off its hinges by the catastrophes of history. People's internal distress was stifled under a blanket of stubbornness: diligence, cleanliness and perseverance merged with this strange mixture of arrogance and a feeling of inferiority.

When lies are told at every turn, when your own experience stands in such stark contrast to the official truth and is thus taken from you, what can you do but fall silent.

And harden yourself, yes. The *Wehrmacht* and SS soldiers had fought together with the Romanian army in Stalingrad, but when they came home the Romanian Germans were criminals while the Romanians were heroes. The minority population was thus hindered from talking about the crimes of the Nazi era, and so from admitting the truth to themselves too. This silencing and hardening also fostered in people a craven, opportunistic attitude towards life. My parents were and remained tamed by fear. The fear of political punishment made them unconditionally servile, incorrigible and cowardly. I experienced it in my family. I was already in the city by this point, working in the factory, and had to endure the harassment of the Securitate, the Romanian secret service: the interrogations, house searches, death threats. My mother was scared for my life, I can understand that. But her fear, born of maternal love, did not just make her politically blind – it also made her insensitive as a mother. And she didn't notice this when she said that I was to blame for my own political persecution and that I was putting the family in danger. She became spiteful, and this feeling was directed at me instead of towards the secret police. Her obedience to the State was doglike; to me, her accusations looked like passive collaboration. She didn't care what reasons I had for not going along with the dictatorship. She wanted to stay in her own safe little world; for us to remain inconspicuous, to perhaps even get ahead, whatever the price. Other people clap along and make money, and you can't keep your gob shut, she'd say. One day you'll be dead in your grave, and what good will it have done you? Is it still some version of a maternal instinct when someone says something like this? She wept as she said it, and she wanted me to comfort her as though I were her mother.

I said I didn't want to learn anything from our family. But I did learn from them. My father's time in the SS was a cautionary example for me. At seventeen, I was the same age as he had been when he swooned over Hitler. And I held this against him. I knew that I too was living in a dictatorship and that I wouldn't be able to hold anything against him if I went along with it.

Does the suffering we experience earn us a moral pass? To this day, I still don't know how I should understand this crass opportunism on my mother's part. Should I downplay it as the cluelessness of a peasant woman? Is it to be explained away by the labour camp or as fear for her child? The facts are there, but what do they have to say? Was this opportunism inevitable?

My mother tried to escape deportation. She hid in a hole in the ground in our neighbours' garden for a week or more at minus twenty degrees. Then she was discovered, dragged out and sent off to the camp in a cattle wagon. This detail – her hiding in a hole in the earth – is dreadful enough, even without the experience of the camp. But did it give her the right to behave so moronically where politics were concerned? As regards my father, I have to imagine very different details. I read Paul Celan's poems and thought: if my father had been sent to a concentration camp when he was a soldier, he would have operated the gas chambers. Or he'd have murdered Celan's parents in Transnistria; you didn't need any gas there. The prisoners lived in shallow holes in the bare fields, and many of them died due to lack of water or food – the rest were shot or beaten to death. I often thought that my mother had to go to the Russian labour camp because of my parents' collective guilt, to counterbalance my father's actions in the war. My goodness, how absurdly is the great sweep of history reflected as guilt and punishment in a single married couple – how unjustly it was distributed between my two parents. And when this distribution took place, they were not even a couple yet, just two people of the same age in a village as small as a thimble on the edge of the world.

From the vantage point of this village and this parental home, I see history everywhere. My father died early from drink; he was only fifty years old. When he was drunk he would still sing Nazi songs with his comrades, even thirty years after the end of the war. The village was small, the weddings big. A lot of boozing went on at the long wooden tables, and you would hear the drunken songs all night long. And the village policeman was Romanian, he had no idea what the men were singing as all these songs were in German – he would just sway along to the music with them. This is why I was not able to view the time these men spent in the SS as a period of youthful folly: they did not revise their positions in any way afterwards.

Long after my father had died and I had left Romania, I visited Coventry. The word coined by Goebbels, '*coventrisieren*', meaning to raze to the ground, hung in the air there, amid the church ruins that reminded me of those haunting scenes. The English wind crashed through the trees, but in my mind I saw the long wooden tables and heard the drunken songs of my village. There are many such places of haunting, and whenever I find them I realise that wherever I go, my father has been there already. Whether I want it or not, my family creeps through the world after me. Or I bring them with me to these places, because you can't leave your head at home. I don't need to feel guilty on my father's behalf, but I do have to give some thought to his actions.

And this thought has led to an interlacing of history on an individual scale and History on a large scale.

Ultimately, the very personal, even the silent and instinctual relationships in every family, also have a political dimension, because they are reacting to the situation that surrounds them. The political has all sorts of psychological effects; it plays a fatal part in everything and everyone. Every family history is also the private imprint of contemporary history.

Of course, the political is always there, but one decides for oneself what one does and does not do – this is personal responsibility. And then one decides for oneself what to learn from any given experience. I believe that you can't make excuses for yourself based on your parents or your ancestry, your childhood happiness or unhappiness, on whether you grew up in a safe or violent environment. Of course you are a result of these things, but you are also the result of your own choices: no one can force you to remain how you were brought up to be. Childhood has a relatively short shelf life. Afterwards, you are responsible for yourself and must raise yourself for the rest of your life, whether you want to or not. How one does this, I don't know. We are so opaque to ourselves. We know the facts, but how they take effect and shape us remains a mystery: our experiences are buried inside us, and we don't know how they make us tick.

You sum up the relationship between stubbornness and dictatorship with the phrase: 'Remaining respectable in private means failing in public.'

Well, I saw what was happening around me. When you are young, you want to show what you can do, to make something of yourself. You have to force yourself to keep quiet during meetings when others are praising the Party and receiving recognition and privileges for it. You have to know: I could recite the Party poem even better than the student standing on stage, but I don't want to stand on stage for that. So then you stay down beneath the stage and are nothing more than a grey average and no one takes any notice of you. As early as secondary school, you have to decide whether or not to do that to yourself: failing in public because you want to remain respectable in private. Remaining true to yourself means holding yourself back; outshining everyone else means betraying yourself. Certainly, no one actually believed in the propaganda. The only question was whether you were going to use it to achieve something in life. It was precisely the highest-ranking Party bigwigs and their children who would get married not just at the registry office but also, secretly, in church – something that was forbidden by the Party. They didn't believe in the Party, just in their own position. And for this they did everything: plotted, blackmailed, denounced, dissembled. They even killed, if they had to.

You 'outshone everyone else' in a different way –
namely, by writing your first book. What changes
did you have to agree to for it to be published?

By the time *Nadirs* finally came out with Kriterion, a Bucharest-based publishing house, after three years and the censorship of several 'editors', its style was mangled and its contents maimed. Whole texts and passages were thrown out and phrasings changed – this was the political face of censorship. Russia, for instance, became 'a distant foreign land'. My first editor wrote poems himself, and the Stalinist style guide was his benchmark for literature. He viewed the intentional repetition of a word or sentence as poor style. When he took something out, he said it had to be 'eliminated'. On top of this he was prudish: anything that was supposedly decadent or vulgar had to go. So the grandmother in my story no longer had mucus in the corner of her eye but 'a sticky something'. When, after all this 'elimination', the book was finally published, I barely cared for it any more. I had written most of it in secret in the factory, in my office, sitting wedged between four accountants, working on my stories instead of translating technical descriptions of hydraulic machines from German into Romanian, which was the job I was supposed to be doing. I worked in a machine factory, but to my mind you were whatever you earned your crust doing – so I was a translator.

I didn't see myself as a writer. I had started to write because my father had died, and because the harassment of the secret service was growing ever more unbearable. I had to make sure that I did actually exist; the hopelessness around me made me feel so afraid. And the fear could be tamed by writing: I didn't want to write 'literature', I wanted to find something to hold on to. When I read books, I always thought that these beautiful sentences, which were more than the sum of their words, knew how life worked for as long as you kept your eyes on them. Yes, just as with the plants back in the valley, so too did these sentences seem to know things that were beyond me. And the sentences I wrote myself were able to say more about me and the village and this childhood of silence than my mouth could. And this enthralled and scared me. These words led to something that I couldn't anticipate. The sentences saw through what I did not understand, perhaps because I had to find words that said more than those you used when speaking out loud, words that were new to me, and to one another. When writing, it was precisely this uncertainty that forced a truth that corresponded to reality – because it did not stop at the world as it *seemed*, but rather went beyond it. And this uncertainty gave me something to hold on to. But I was writing words in fear. It was like me eating those plants: I had a hunger for words. I was inventing real life in an unreal way; it was never a one-to-one match, but much more precise for this very reason. And there was always the fantasy that, in the care of these sentences, I might come to know how to live a little better. The sentences by no means spared me, but the work I had to do to produce them gave me something to hold on to.

I never imagined back then that *Nadirs* could be published in Germany. I got anxious when I heard the news.

At the time, the secret service already had you in
its sights, you had to be exceedingly careful.

To edit the book again, I met up with my West Berlin editor in the Poiana Braşov ski resort in the Carpathian Mountains. This was supposed to be a conspiratorial operation: we were pretending to be tourists on a skiing holiday; the secret service shouldn't find out that we were meeting. It was the beginning of the ski season, but only on paper. The sun had been shining like crazy on the Carpathians during the early winter that year, and the air was as warm as at the tail end of summer. There wasn't a speck of snow, and there were no tourists; it was just the two of us in the hotel. The editor had brought along a suitcase full of candles and tin cans. And I had brought along the manuscript. Unfortunately, our rooms were not next to each other. We met 'by accident' in the restaurant and drank coffee. When the editor returned to her room, half the candles and tin cans had already vanished from her suitcase. She knocked on my door and asked after the manuscript. I checked on it. Luckily, it was still there. We could never leave the manuscript alone in the room again and under no circumstances could we work on the edit in our rooms. We realised that we were not here incognito. We had to agree on a secret knock, so we would recognise one another. The editor knocked on the door with her knuckles, two long beats, three short ones. That's easy to remember, she said. I wasn't so sure. Then she repeated the knock and accompanied it by saying 'Ho-Ho-Ho-Chi-Minh'. I was horrified, I was up to my ears in Ho Chi Minh and the Cultural Revolution. Good grief. No, I can't do that knock, I said. Then think of other words to go with it, she said, we don't have to change the rhythm. But the rhythm was taken; whatever I thought up, all I could hear was Ho Chi Minh.

And this was just the beginning of the mountain edit. We began working outside and sat ourselves down like two lizards on a warm slab of stone on the mountainside. Until all of a sudden we heard an ear-splitting clatter. We looked up the mountainside and started running. There were soldiers standing above us, pushing iron drums down the hill. They were zigzagging towards us, faster than we could run – we had to jump out of their way. We would have been crushed had one of those drums hit us. We made it to a ski lift and hid behind the cabin. The drums had rolled just past us into the valley, and the soldiers had vanished. I think this attack with the drums was pure chance, entertainment for brutal, bored soldiers rather than anything intentional. Ceauşescu had countless hunting grounds in the Carpathians, entire forests were restricted areas and there were soldiers stationed everywhere. We stayed sitting in a hollow and worked on our edit. Then we went to have dinner in the hotel restaurant. As we were eating, around fifty East Asian men came in, they were all wearing the same dark jackets and trousers. It was probably a state visit, a delegation from North Korea.

Ceauşescu often visited North Korea; Kim Il-Sung was his role model. The waiters had been expecting the delegation: in the middle of the room, they'd arranged the furniture to form one long table. The men took their seats. The group included two Romanians; one of them gave a theatrical speech about hospitality and Socialism. The other translated this rather curtly, and they raised their glasses to hospitality. The soup was already being served, and music started to play over the restaurant's loudspeakers: Romanian popular hits. The men drank schnapps, and it kept getting louder in the hall.

I suggested we go to one of our rooms. The editor asked if we could stay a bit longer. She said she would like to dance with one of the men. She wanted to go over to the long table and invite one of them to dance. Don't you dare, I said, otherwise you'll have to dance with all of them one after the other through to tomorrow morning. She wanted me to join in, of course. Never, I said. Then the two of us should at least dance with each other, she said, because she felt like dancing. By doing that we would be suggesting that we want to dance with them, I said, and if they invite us to dance and we refuse, there will be problems. I was aghast that, after her Ho Chi Minh knock, she now wanted to dance with the Communists. We were living in completely different worlds: what I saw as threatening she saw as exotic. When she got stuck in the hotel lift, she knew this was deliberate, and felt as if she were being imprisoned; she was more afraid than I was. But when a situation was genuinely risky, she didn't understand a thing. It was probably equally trying for both of us: I was an Eastern child of the State and jaded by harassment, she was an ideological '68er from the West.

And all of this in the Carpathians. I had agreed to it; I thought it would help our conspiracy. But without any snow we were more conspicuous there than we would have been in any city.

I was out of place anyway in those mountains, the sky enclosed in stone, the cliff faces stretching up above us like windowless barracks. You climbed up the mountainside with your feet above your head; with the clouds underneath your feet. I felt disoriented, dizzy from our imbecilic idea of posing as skiers and the notion that such a place would serve our conspiracy.

Because of our plan, we had arrived at the hotel separately. I had already been there for a few hours, and was waiting for the editor's bus. I walked up and down in front of the hotel and saw hollyhocks growing up the side of the wall; they still had half-wilted blossom on them, a velvety black more beautiful than I had ever seen in our garden. I plucked some dried seeds off the stems and took them home; I wanted to plant them in our garden in the spring, when I would drive out to the country again. I put them in a drawer in my kitchen. When spring came, however, the bag with the seeds was gone. When I asked my husband if he had put the little blue bag with the hollyhock seeds away somewhere else, he said: I've been sprinkling the grains from the little blue bag in our soup, I thought they were a spice.

It was a shame, the velvety black mountain hollyhocks were so beautiful partly because, like me, they were themselves not at home in the mountains – they were neither at home nor themselves, in fact. I could feel it. My instinct from the river valley was still working. I would have liked to plant such a foreign plant, which walked around at night, in our garden, and hope that it spread, from one garden to another, throughout the whole village.

If one compares the last, authorised version of Nadirs* *with the one that came into being in the Carpathians†, one sees how much your German editor also interfered with the text. There are some particularly fine, sensual passages missing, which are among the most beautiful in the book. Did you have any fights during the edit, or arguments at least?*

The edit was easy: I didn't object when something was taken out, I didn't care a bit. I often get asked why. The texts were about this village, as small as a thimble on the edge of the world. And Romania as a whole, with its insane dictatorship and its gloomy poverty, was itself on the edge of the world. Every day, I desperately needed the beauty of these sentences because I was writing in order to find something to hold on to in the face of misery, not because I wanted to create 'literature'. I had been reading books and magazines from the West for years, and there was no censorship there. I was convinced that the editor's changes had purely literary motives – and as far as aesthetics were concerned, somebody from the West would know better than I did. And who would be interested in a prudish German minority and a dictatorship at the edge of the world, I thought. If a book like this were to be published in the West, it shouldn't be too long, otherwise nobody would buy it.

---

*   *Niederungen* (Munich: Hanser Verlag, 2010)
†   *Niederungen* (Berlin: Rotbuch Verlag, 1984)

*Some stories with direct political references such
as 'Die Meinung', 'Inge' and 'Herr Wultschmann'*
were not included.*

The stories that were left out are less poetic, and more
directly political. They are similar to one another; they're
ironic, making their points through repetition. Perhaps the
editor did not like this type of text in and of itself, or she
thought that those stories were simply not good from a
literary perspective, or perhaps there were, consciously or
subliminally, entirely different reasons.

*In contrast, stories such as 'The Swabian Bath' and
'About German Moustaches and Hair Parts' seem
much less controversial, and it is precisely these that
earned you the hatred of the* Landsmannschaft,
*the Homeland Association of Banat Swabians, who
hounded you unwaveringly for a long time, even
after you had emigrated.*

The *Landsmannschaft* found *Nadirs* outrageous, scan-
dalous. These people knew only penny dreadfuls and
homeland literature, in which the Banat region in Romania
was the most beautiful place in the world and in which
'Germanness' was a virtue, signalling diligence, cleanliness,
tradition. You love your homeland and your homeland
loves you. It's where your roots are, it's where you belong.

---

* These stories are not included in the existing English translation
of *Nadirs* either, as this was translated from the book's West
Berlin edition, published by Rotbuch Verlag – the edition Herta
Müller was working on in the Carpathians – rather than from
the original Romanian edition published by Kriterion.

The earth is fertile, the sun is golden; this is how things should be. The *Landsmannschaft*'s headquarters had always been in Munich. Its officials had been living in the free world for decades, but projected their homeland on to Romania. It was an abstract homeland, a picture book full of carved wooden gates, ornately gabled houses, brass bands and folk dances. But they weren't interested in the fact that the wooden gates and gabled roofs of these villages were now located in a dictatorship. Their homeland ideology didn't need to grapple with their actual homeland and what daily life was like in a totalitarian state. To this day, they wallow in the abstract idea of their homeland and this distant ownership of it.

When these arbiters of the homeland read that the Earth was gobbling us up in the villages, that their homeland stood like a three-hundred-year-old box in the landscape, that there was more boozing and suicide than happiness, they became vicious. I had besmirched their homeland and their Germanness. I hadn't intended to annoy the *Landsmannschaft* in Munich or my compatriots in Romania. That was what the village was like to me, even before I left it. During my childhood, in particular. I used to think that we were in the lonely, windy dirt of the fields, on the tasselled fringes of the world – the main body of the carpet was made out of asphalt, and it was in the city. On the asphalt, Death can't creep round your ankles. To me, the word 'homeland' carried different connotations to those in the songs: it consisted of prowling plants, of the hereafter up in the sky, of your skin scorching and freezing and the bleak exhaustion of our village grief, of our heavy old props and tools. That was why, even as a child, I always wanted to move to the city. I thought that in the village everyone was old; that people were born old. If you wanted to grow young, you had to get out of the village. And when I arrived in the city, my insecurity and feelings of inferiority gave me heart palpitations, but still I felt that escaping the village was a stroke of fortune. From the first day on, I could no longer imagine ever going back. Nonetheless, I felt a home-sickness, perhaps not in my brow, just on the gum, because the city spoke Romanian and I did not know the language. What helped overcome this most was reading books and, with time, the Romanian that I slowly acquired through daily life. Comparisons opened up; Romanian words wandered into my German. '*Cer*', in Romanian, means 'sky', or 'heaven', while an official request is '*cerere*'. So an official request in Romania is a petition to the heavens – in other words, there's no point in making it at all. Such thoughts kept occurring to me. The more surreal they seemed, the more accurately they described reality. When I was summoned to an interrogation, I would try out all sorts of rhymes on the way there. For example: 'My fatherland is an apple core, 'twixt sickle and star we pitch and yaw'. Yes, when you had to go to an interrogation, you were summoned to the fatherland. The rhyme knew the score. I noticed during these mental exercises that the poetic is real and that its shimmering language is the best way of highlighting how shitty life is. First, I freed myself from the village by reading, and then by writing, because my invented sentences were able to articulate what my child-hood had looked like better than I could ever have said aloud. And it unsettled me to see how the sentences were showing me that this village upbringing, just thirty kilo-metres away, was of no use to me any more in the city – that I had to unlearn the ideas and opinions of the village.

> *The* Landsmannschaft *evidently took the literary*
> *sentences to be real; they read the stories as though*
> *they were reports.*

In *Nadirs*, the father is a Nazi and has helped fill grave-yards all over the world. But this father was no literary figure for the *Landsmannschaft*: they knew him; a part of them lived inside him. And on top of that came the poetic devices. The poplars look like knives. They read that literally too, and therefore it was not just the people, but everything about their villages, even the trees, that I had defamed. That it is possible to love things you cannot bear, that love and tedium can be the same, that sometimes things are in between and put together differently to how you might ordinarily describe them – all of this was beyond the imagination of the homeland ideologues. The *Landsmannschaft* was a kind of Ministry of Feelings for the Homeland. Whatever did not fit into their register of feelings was viewed as 'fouling your own nest'. And I was exhibited as a 'nest fouler' in the *Landsmannschaft* newspapers; I was even defamed as a Securitate informer. The feelings you were allowed to have for your homeland were clichés, kitschy and prefabricated. They were dishonest, and therefore as unfit for literary purposes as the Party's regulations would have been. There were in fact two Ministries of Feelings: one was governed by the Securitate, the Romanian regime, the other by the *Landsmannschaft* in Munich, which didn't have a critical word to say about the dictatorship either. It wasn't until I read my file from the Bucharest Gauck Commission that I understood why that decade had taken the shape it did. The *Landsmannschaft* collaborated with the Securitate; they had been infiltrated by informers; their hatred and the assignments they were given by the Securitate had helped the dictatorship counterfeit reality for decades. They never expected the fall of the regime, nor that access to the secret service files would be opened up. Now, the entanglement of the *Landsmannschaft* with a criminal secret service is quite awkward for the homeland photo album. People in the *Landsmannschaft* have since kept quiet about this topic.

*You always stress that, when writing, our lived
experience is carried over into a craft in which the
primary issue is no longer day or night, village or city,
but rather noun and verb, beat and sound – that
reality can only be captured in a roundabout way.*

A roundabout way, because there is no such thing as 'the right way' when you are writing. No, I think the roundabout way is the right way. Because, in order to write a sentence, I must sheer away from the semantic habits of words; I choose them based on their rhythm and sound, and they become unexpectedly accurate and say what I did not know I knew for the first time. And this new language does not contradict the facts – on the contrary, it makes them clearer. After all, it is indeed a fact that my fatherland, with its sickle and star, is an apple core. I don't know how the words accomplish this, but the sentence comes out sparkling, saying far more than the content of its words. But how is one supposed to explain the iridescence of a sentence to an ideologue of the homeland or fatherland? You can't negotiate with ideologues; they have no need for aesthetics. Instead of desperate beauty, they need kitsch and their own stubborn, worthy dogmatism. Only one rule applies for the homeland inspectors, the arbiters of who 'we' are: things must be the way they have always been, so that they stay this way forever.

But literature can find no place in a world that is so sure of itself. And there was no room at all for writing, as an activity that was to be taken seriously, was there?

The people I grew up with didn't even acknowledge reading to be a worthwhile activity, let alone writing. Only those who were too lazy to work read books. Reading was also viewed as unhealthy. It ruined your eyes and, even worse, it affected your nerves. If you read too much, you might become *profound*. And on top of this came mistrust: quite rightly, nobody believed what was written in the papers each day. If you caught someone lying you would say: you're lying like you're in print.

In our snowed-in village, my grandfather would read the Brockhaus Encyclopaedia like a novel. He would pick up the Encyclopaedia, start at A and then keep going until the winter was over. He knew all sorts of things as a result. And once the snow was gone he would put the Encyclopaedia away, right at the back of the cupboard, up at the top behind the fur hats stuffed with tobacco leaves. The tobacco was to protect them from moths. In the dark silence of the cupboard, the fur hats and the Encyclopaedia would wait for the next winter. The fur hats were still eaten bald by the moths; they looked like they were made of bone. But the Encyclopaedia remained intact and smelt of tobacco all winter. The next year, my grandfather would start reading from A again, as if he had forgotten everything during his work over the summer.

My father never picked up an encyclopaedia. Nor did my mother or grandmother – they would knit socks in the winter. All of us wore only hand-knitted sheep-wool socks. We would buy a big sack of wool, which looked like a huge ball of dirty cotton wool, and then we had to comb it out: there were little stones in it, grass, dried sheep dung. It wasn't until it had been cleaned that you could wash it, dry it, spin it, twist it into skeins. Then we'd take it to the city to be dyed, and only once this was done would it be wound from skeins into balls of wool. *Then* you could knit socks. The roles were clearly assigned: the woman dealt with the socks, the man with the Encyclopaedia.

There was another book in the house that was always kept hidden right at the bottom of the cupboard: the Doctor Book. It had a black cover and was as thick as two volumes of the Encyclopaedia. The Doctor Book contained descriptions of all illnesses and how to treat them at home. Anyone who read the Doctor Book had no need for a doctor, which was why our neighbours would often borrow it. Even our female neighbours would read the Doctor Book. Unlike books intended only for pleasure, here was a volume that made you healthy again. Illnesses were kept secret among the grown-ups; they would never reveal the shame of a disease to each other. If a neighbour borrowed the Doctor Book, you would never ask them what they were looking for information about. In the village, illnesses could well be punishments from Our Lord for something or other. My grandfather would enter into a notebook who had borrowed the Doctor Book on what day and in how many days they would bring it back, like a librarian. Children weren't allowed to read it.

In summer, people seldom borrowed the Doctor Book,

as nobody had any time for illnesses. Everyone was out of the house – outside in the field, in the yard, in the garden – far away from the silence of the cupboard. On these days, I would take out the Doctor Book. I would open a narrow crack in the blinds, enough to let in a bit of light, but not so much that it would be noticeable from the outside, and I would lay the Doctor Book down on the carpet and go straight to the page showing the naked body. You could open the body up. There were two rib doors beneath the neck, and underneath those two belly doors. The chest and genitals were both female and male; the body was at once man and woman. You could empty out the chest and the belly, and I would lay out the many organs next to each other on the carpet. They were in different colours, but all in pastel shades, and they were all numbered. I would assemble a woman's breasts with male genitalia. Then the other way round. Or I'd put the heart in the belly, and the gall bladder in the neck. I couldn't play for too long, because it took time to put all the organs away in their right places again. They all had to fit in just so, to ensure that the chest and belly would close again.

The organs were of course already warped from having been rearranged so often. My grandfather knew that the naked body had not been worn down merely from having been lent out. He would say: you've been at the Doctor Book again, haven't you? And he would put the emphasis on 'again'. And I would deny it and wait for my next opportunity to open it up.

Perhaps it wasn't a bad idea to forbid me from reading the Doctor Book. After all, the multicoloured organs haunted me. I imagined I could see how the organs were packed inside every neighbour, dog or turkey in the village. I was overcome with fear and revulsion because I thought that the organs took on the colour of everything we ate: white from bread, blue from plums, yellow from sugar melons. And I imagined our organs were jumbled around each day, that they would slip into a different arrangement while we were working, walking or sleeping. And although I had studied the womb in the woman's belly in the Doctor Book, I continued to believe that children were brought along by a stork. Not that it would fly down from the air; I thought the stork nested inside the belly. There was a little picture in the Doctor Book of a womb with an embryo inside it, pale and crooked like a bean sprouting in the earth. I thought it wasn't a bean sprout but a little stork, and when it grew it turned into a child. Nobody doubted the Doctor Book, it was proof that, as well as being human beings, we were also animals, plants and objects. That the organs inside us were in league with the secret of time, which gathers our breaths like glass beads on a string. So that the material of the body and of the village were even more eerily enmeshed with one another. I think that what I gleaned from the Doctor Book made me feel even more lost – in the cornfield and in the valley with the cows, at the dining table with my parents and at night in bed, in my dark room. The grown-ups said that if you killed a swallow, the cows would give you red milk. This was how surreal and yet entirely commonplace our superstitions were. They had this dark, magical breadth, full of word wizardry. In an inscrutable logic, the milk inside the cow senses the death of the swallow and is coloured by its blood. Cause and consequence are mixed up here in such a startlingly new way, just as they are in truly great literature.

I have to say one more thing about the Doctor Book: when my grandfather died, it disappeared. My mother never wrote down whom she had lent it to. She forgot, and the Doctor Book was never returned.

In the winter, when the villagers were looking up their diseases and your grandfather was reading the Encyclopaedia, the village was even more isolated than usual: the train would get stuck, the paths would hide in the snow, and the only connection to the world was the postman who occasionally came by.

He would bring the newspaper, and if my grandfather wasn't careful, I would tear off a scrap and eat it. I liked the taste of the grey-white, porous paper and of the ink: a little spicy, bitter and salty. I also liked to eat mouldy fruit, the very last plums that were still hanging on the branches after the leaves had all fallen off. On late, hot summer days, the plum peels would wither like old skin and would become covered in a green-white mould, and their flesh would ferment a little. The taste was rotten-sweet, and very spicy. My grandmother, my father's mother, always used to make rotten cheese. It was literally called 'rotten cheese'. She would tamp it into an earthen pot and leave it to stand for about ten days. We wouldn't eat it until it had become glassy and had a bold, sharp taste. Sour, bitter, spicy, rotten – these are the tastes I have always liked, nothing sweet. To this day I still can't eat ripe apricots, but I like the bitter green ones that make your mouth furry. This is also what sloe berries taste like. You have to wait for at least one frost in the autumn. My grandmother who made the rotten cheese would also pick sloe berries and make sloe berry compote to go with roast meat in the winter. This was what poor people would eat: those who had no land of their own, no trees. There were sloe bushes between all the fields. The graveyard fence was lined with sloe berries, too. The dead are inside this fruit, I used to think, when I picked the black beads. It disgusted me, but I still ate them. Perhaps that was precisely why I ate them – I could have picked fruit from another patch, there were enough sloe bushes around. Wild fruit tastes very good: crab apples, wild pears, blackberries, medlars. I was in Edenkoben once, in the early spring, and I walked through the vineyards to the next village. There were still patches of snow on the ground and, between the vines, three or four people were cutting down freshly grown thistles. They were still frozen, finely barbed leaves coated in a layer of glass. I thought maybe the people had rabbits at home. I spoke to them: they came from the Baltic states and knew that you can eat thistles once the snow has melted.

People had newspaper subscriptions because you needed paper – it wasn't there to be read, it was used for wrapping things, wiping, covering things up. Not just in the village, in the city too. I have already told the story of how a passer-by on the street covered the dead man's face with his newspaper. Paper is light and keeps things warm, you would use it to line your shoes. No other kind of paper was available anywhere in the country. There was talk of a paper crisis – though this was also a pretext for censorship. I would take home used paper from the factory, on one side were the accounting department's lists and numbers, but I could write on the reverse side. During the final years of the Ceauşescu regime, the immiseration had reached such depths that even in the State-owned factories people were using newspaper as toilet paper. In the school I taught in before leaving the country, the schoolchildren had to cut up newspapers into hand-sized pieces. But, given all the Party worship and the cult of personality, it would have been fatal, treasonous even, if Ceauşescu's image had been degraded by being used as toilet paper. The schoolchildren who were responsible for the toilet paper had to look through the newspapers with the utmost care and cut them up in such a way that no body part of Ceauşescu's ended up in the toilet. And not just his face: no ear or trouser leg or shoe of his either. The whole thing with cutting up the toilet paper was tricky, but unavoidable, because there had been no toilet paper for sale in the whole country for years.

You were saying earlier that people had clear roles in the village: socks for the women, the Encyclopaedia for the man. And this was the case even though the women worked just as hard in the fields as the men, and beat the children just as much at home?

Yes, village life assigned completely different roles to men and women, and they didn't change very much over time. Many tasks were allocated according to physical strength: the men would chop wood, cut hay, lug sacks and slaughter pigs; the women would clean shoes, turn the hay and slaughter chickens. Things weren't very different in the city, either. The only areas where anything changed were those where machines were involved. A woman in the factory could also be a crane driver. But mayors, Party secretaries, police officers or nightwatchmen were all men, both in the city and in the country. There were very concrete ideas behind this: the mayor and the Party secretary need to have authority. The police officer and the night-watchman need physical strength if a burglar comes along. These were unwritten rules. Romania had a peasant mentality, even in the cities. The Party bigwigs mostly came from the poorest areas. They were the sons of farmers, and had built their careers by adapting to the requisite ideology. There were so many of them that they had no need to change their mentality; they were in the majority, and so their offices and administrations became just like them. Provinciality and prudishness were a good fit for Stalinist ideas, and brutality was required in order to intimidate and incapacitate people in the reprisals that had to be meted out every day. Even afterwards, in its post-Stalinist form, Socialism remained nationalistic, narrow-minded, prudish and heavy-handed to the end. And it was hostile, not just for ideological reasons, but also because of the ignorance of its functionaries. Incompetence and power make for a terrible concoction. Behind every government door sat a smoothly polished deadbeat with a Party badge on his lapel, a gold rock on his finger and a commanding tone in his mouth. The archetypal Socialist functionary really was abhorrent from the crown of his head to the tips of his shoes. I was so often humiliated by them. I despised them so much. There must be something essential about this type, because even nowadays – I mean twenty-five years later – when I see the Chinese Party Congress or the Russian duma on the television, I see the same type of person, right down to the tiniest detail. The arrogant cruelty of Communist functionaries – they might come from the most different and remote corners of the world, but their body language is the same. As is their demeanour, which lies somewhere between sleazy and brutish. Whether they are Asian, European or South American, it's as if they have all graduated from the same cadet school.

To return once more to the roles of men and women, I think that beating the children was parcelled out too. The men would beat the sons, the women would beat the daughters. My father never hit me, but not because he was a gentle soul – it was simply my mother's duty. Even beating had its unwritten rules. Perhaps humiliation required an unsettling intimacy in order to be more effective. A father hitting his son humiliates him differently compared to if it was his mother doing so. And likewise, a mother hitting her daughter wounds her differently than if her father were to do it.

The Clothes of Socialism

*You started to write because you were in an existential
quandary: you could no longer see a way out, and
so you tried, through your sentences, to get a hold
on things — a hold that your lived experience could
no longer offer you.*

I found myself facing two situations simultaneously: in the
factory, the secret service's harassment was growing increasingly intolerable, while in the village my father lay dying,
and did indeed pass away after a few weeks. During his
final days, he was in the district hospital in the city, which
was diagonally across from my block of flats. I visited him
every day and watched his body slowly disappear; every
day he would look more like a white-beaked bird. In the
deliquescence of his body, the whole village showed itself
once more: they were both made of this silent, sad material.
My relationship with my father, if we can even call it a relationship, consisted of irreconcilable conflicts, yet I carried
his death around with me for a very long time. It's not so
much that I suffered from it, it was more that I grappled
with it — there is a difference. During the daily harassment
I endured from my managers and the secret service, my

childhood increasingly forced itself upon me. Perhaps I wanted or needed to distract myself with other thoughts, with an earlier time, because there was no way out of the wretchedness of the present moment. My childhood would not leave me in peace; the whole village quivered in the mirror of my mind. I could no longer make a distinction between my life before and my life now. I was compelled to ask myself all sorts of confused questions: why am I here in this factory? What am I when I'm here? Why am I at the mercy of this despotism? I also wondered how much of the village remained in me after all these years, after my time in secondary school, my studies in the city. I still watched the plants in the gardens and parks of the city, and separated them out into those that had remained true to themselves – poplars, birches, phlox and dahlias – and those that had defected to the State, such as cedar, boxwood, red carnations and gladioli. But this was a habit from village life. I still looked for four-leaved clover in the grassy verge of the narrow streets on my way home from the factory. This was a village habit, too. I didn't think for a moment that the clover would bring me luck and change my circumstances. It was clear to me that the luck of four-leaved clover begins and ends with the act of finding it. And yet I looked for it anyway. You see, I was looking for a way to distract myself from the harassment, but also from the loneliness. Perhaps the village was not coming back to me because of the death of my father, but because of my great loneliness in the factory. My isolation was no side effect, but rather what the secret service intended. When you are being persecuted, fear and loneliness belong together. People avoid you. Your colleagues sidestep you; they don't want to be seen with you, for fear of ending up in the secret service's sights themselves. This hurts. You are no longer good enough for the others. You are harassed from above and discriminated against from below. In short, the more you are harassed, the lonelier you become. I started writing out of loneliness. This period marked my second great loneliness – the first was when I was living in the village, when I didn't yet know the word 'lonely' because it does not exist in our dialect. During my second loneliness I did know the word, both in German and in Romanian, but what use was it to me?

You had been turned out of your office and would
spend the whole day on the staircase.

There's a backstory to this. I had been sharing an office with four accountants for three years. But now our factory – which specialised in tractors and wire mesh – was starting to reverse-engineer Citroën designs. They hired another two ladies to do translations and opened an entirely new so-called records office. The two ladies, one for English and one for French, were daughters of the *nomenklatura*, the bureaucratic elite of the Communist regime – the English lady in fact was the daughter-in-law of the city's second-highest-ranking secret service agent.

I had to move into the records office with these two ladies. However, when we received visits from foreign experts, I had to leave the room for as long as their discussions were taking place. And there was a secret compartment in our cupboard where they kept the records of these discussions, for which I did not have a key. Both of these ladies were working for the secret service, there was no doubt about this. I just didn't understand at first why I had been forced to move into their office. It wasn't until the secret service blackmailed me that I understood that they had been set on turning me into an informer all along, ever since they'd transferred me. The secret service and management evidently never imagined that I would refuse. But I did refuse, and so I was of no use to their records office. I begged in vain to return to my previous office – but they needed me to disappear from the factory altogether. They thought all they needed to do was harass me enough and I would leave of my own accord. Two men came to the records office, and the ladies 'happened' not to be present. I knew one of them: a short, weedy engineer who would often drop in to talk to the ladies. He had a metallic voice and he paid them slimy compliments. He laughed brashly and far too much. Like a butler to an important guest, he was now accompanying a huge blond guy, who introduced himself by name as the captain of the secret service. Our brash 'engineer' now seemed over-cautious and subservient. The factory didn't even fall under the 'blond visitor's' purview; the captain worked for the literature bureau of the secret service. These agents often helped themselves to fake names, but I had described the way he looked to Romanian friends and learnt that he had interrogated many writers and sometimes beaten them up. I was involved in the *Aktionsgruppe Banat*,* and so I knew rock musicians, theatre people – it was a small city after all. They probably did want me to inform on others at the factory, but also on these artistic circles. When I refused to write a statement declaring myself to be an informer the captain said, we'll

---

* A literary society founded by members of the German-speaking Banat Swabian minority. The group fought for freedom of speech under the dictatorship.

throw you in the river. It wasn't just the size of him that made him so intimidating, he also had these piercing blue eyes. They looked empty, twinkled like rhinestones – they barely had pupils. Well, they must have been there somewhere, but you couldn't see them. Perhaps they had swum round to the back of his eyeballs.

You refused with the words 'It's not in my nature,'
which further aggravated the situation.

The secret service agent had not been expecting me to say no. He had misjudged me, and now felt betrayed by me. When, after the word *'colaborez'*, I refused to continue writing what the captain was dictating to me, he tore up the sheet of paper and threw it on the floor. He took a deep breath, but when I then said it's not in my nature, he cursed, grabbed a vase full of tulips from the table and threw it against the wall. Then it must have occurred to him that he would have to report this failed recruitment to his boss: he gathered up the shreds of paper from the floor and stuck them into his briefcase. You'll regret this, he said, and left abruptly – he didn't even take the time to close the door behind him. It was as if he was running away. I was, I think, calm, as if absent from myself. I went to fetch a dustpan and brush and swept up the shards, as if everything would be fine once they were gone.

I was relieved that the secret service now knew that I wouldn't cooperate in any way, that I didn't want them to give me a chance to prove myself, that I stood to lose nothing, no matter what they took from me. Becoming an informer, however – that would have been a betrayal of myself. This was the only outcome I viewed as bad, and it hadn't happened. Even hitting rock bottom reassured me in some way: how could I fall any lower?

When the two colleagues I shared an office with resurfaced, they knew what had taken place. They thought I was insane. Do you realise who you're playing with, one of them asked. She could call the captain if I had changed my mind. I said nothing, nor was she expecting an answer. They're going to crush you, she said.

And this is exactly what they tried to do: little by little, the factory became a witches' cauldron.

I arrived at work the next morning at half past six and the porter sent me to the director. With him were the Party secretary and the head of the trade union. And they told me that I was dispensable, lazy, incompetent, that I should look for a different job. From that point on, this procedure would take place every morning; at the porter's behest, I would go straight to the director as soon as I arrived for work and let myself be insulted. Before I was allowed to leave, they would ask the same question, with the same wording each time: have you found another job? Then I would say, also with the same wording each time: I haven't looked for one, I like it in the factory, I want to stay here till I retire. I said this very calmly, without a trace of irony. It gratified me, it was a tiny, helpless, sadistic gesture, because every time I said it the director would hit the ceiling.

Then they transferred me, as an unqualified worker, to the wire mesh department. This was in a different neighbourhood. The director thought I would finally resign. I stayed there for about two weeks; it was full of weaving looms and spools of wire as big as cisterns. No one would even have dreamt of letting me anywhere near a loom. Instead, I would just wander around the hall. I was embarrassed; I knew that I could do nothing here. It wasn't my fault, but still I was embarrassed; the people here worked hard, and I didn't have a clue about weaving wire, I was of no use. A compassionate work brigade leader kept giving me new piles of notebooks in which to draw lines and label rubrics. The wire weavers' piece rate was entered into the notebooks. Nobody asked me how I had ended up there, even though all I did was stand around and draw lines in notebooks all day. I don't know whether the brigade leader knew, whether everybody knew, or whether nobody did. You didn't dawdle when weaving wire for a piece rate; the workers paid me no attention. Then, one day, the brigade leader sent me back to the records office.

A few days later, I open the door to my office and there's someone sitting at my desk. It's polite to knock before walking into someone else's office, he said. He was an engineer. The hefty dictionaries I used for translating were lying outside in the corridor, next to my notebooks and pens. I had no office any more. But on no account could I go home, or they would have been able to fire me for unexcused absence. I had to be particularly punctilious at this time.

The situation was unbearable, but you still didn't want to leave?

I wanted them to tell me why I had to leave. For them to at least say: you can't stay here any longer because you're refusing to work for the secret service. I asked them why they were being so cowardly. If they were in the right, why didn't they state their real reasons? Why didn't they admit how much they cared about the secret service here in the factory? Why this secretiveness? After all, they could openly make it a condition that you had to work for the secret service, if that was how things were. But perhaps this wasn't how things were after all, perhaps it was still illegal for the secret service to interfere in this way? Why did they pretend to be deaf when anyone said the words 'secret service'? After all, it was surely a pleasure for them to discuss the achievements of the secret service . . . They already knew my absurd monologue as well as I knew their invectives. They would stare at me coldly, they would scream at me.

I would have to go if they threw me out, but I wanted the reasons at least not to be bogus. I had to behave with strict discipline every day, so that nothing could be held against me. I couldn't arrive a second late in the morning. I would go back to my desk when everyone else was drawing out their lunch break. I continued to go to the factory even when I no longer had an office. And I would stay for the whole eight hours. I couldn't leave a second earlier.

My friend Jenny cleared a corner of her desk for me to work from. There were design draughtsmen, desks and drawing tables in her office. But this only lasted a few days. One morning, she was waiting for me in front of her door and she told me she couldn't let me work at her desk any more, that I could no longer come into their office. Her colleagues had told her I was an informer.

This marked the beginning of my time on the staircase. Where was I supposed to go? I had to stay inside the factory, and I had to be somewhere where people would see me, so that no one could claim that I was bunking off work, that I wasn't even on the premises. My friend's office was on the top floor. I moved my dictionaries and notebooks to the staircase between the floors and then I didn't know what to do. So I sat myself down next to my things. I sat down on my handkerchief – I think this was important. I did so because the staircase was made out of concrete, because it was cold and dirty, but then I just continued this way. I would sit down every day on my handkerchief, as if it were itself a room. The handkerchief became a piece of private property. I wasn't sitting exposed on the staircase, I was enclosed within the bounds of my handkerchief, as if I were in my own room. My handkerchief office was a state of mind. Up until the moment I was dismissed, I spent eight hours each day with dictionaries and notebooks on my lap. The office workers had to use the staircase of course, and it wasn't that wide, so they would walk right past me, upstairs and downstairs, and the clatter of their shoes would reach me before they passed by and would echo long after. Some of them said hello and others didn't, but nobody asked me anything. And I began to doubt: perhaps I only *thought* that I was sitting there on the staircase, when in reality I no longer existed at all. And sometimes I would think of Veronika waiting for her missing husband, waiting for the wind at the alley gate. But my friend did come by during the lunch break. I was no longer allowed into her office, so she would come to me on the staircase, and we really did eat together. It was all she could do. And it meant an awful lot to me, the fact that at least one person in the factory trusted me and saw just how ludicrous defamation could be. Because the staircase was one thing, but when I went down to the factory floor to ask the workers about a word, people would whistle after me, and I was called a Party whore and an informer. It was a dreadful time. How was I to explain what was going on to dozens of people? I was being accused of doing the exact thing that I had refused to do. And in order to achieve this, they had activated the informers in the factory. So those doing precisely what I was being accused of doing were now making themselves look innocent by directing suspicions at me. I did not want to become one of them, and they publicly denounced me for it. I would never have dreamt up such perfidy, but it worked. My friend was at pains to amuse us both, she called the captain 'the blond visitor'. If you remember, he had said you'll regret this as he hurriedly left the office. But no, I never regretted it for a moment. What I did had been right at the time, and it remained right. My only mistake was thinking that I had hit rock bottom. Perhaps I had at that point – but I continued to sink further each day after the staircase became my office. And after the calumny began, there were no limits to how far I could fall. I was tumbling into a bottomless pit.

There were stray cats living on the factory grounds, between the pipes, the wire coils, the stacks of wood and boxes. I had begun watching them more often, since sitting on the staircase. Sometimes they carried a pigeon in their mouth, sometimes a rat. They were scruffy and gaunt, but they had no enemies here in the factory. I envied them, I would have gladly swapped places with them.

There is nothing one can do when one is exposed to such defamation. Was your friend the only person who knew what was going on? Were you completely isolated otherwise?

I would have liked to tell a few more colleagues why things were the way they were. But what good would it have done? Would they even have believed me? And how was I to tell them? They didn't want to know anything; they never asked a single question. The two ladies from the records office avoided me, they were careful not to bump into me or to visit me on the staircase. And even if they had, what were they supposed to say? Whether or not people had asked them why I had to leave our office, I don't know. But if they did talk to the others about me, it certainly won't have been to my advantage. They won't have mentioned my non-compliance, nor will they have understood it. For them, it went without saying that you would work for the secret service. And it was beyond comprehension that you would do yourself injury. They weren't malicious, they didn't view my refusal as treason, they simply didn't believe in anything: not in any form of Socialism, nor any party. They wanted to rise up into the *nomenklatura*, that was all. They got special food, special doctors, were awarded privileges by all the authorities, could buy Western cosmetics and clothing. They were spared the yellow, rancid bacon wrapped in newspaper, the watered-down alcohol, the dust-grey clothes from our domestic factories – these joys were the preserve of the proletariat.

The weedy 'engineer' didn't even have to lie when he paid the two ladies compliments. They were the most beautiful women in the factory, they were physically stunning and expensively dressed. The sons of the *nomenklatura* always married beautiful women, it was one of the perks of their status. And for the women, their beauty was their capital: they invested it, they weren't going to let the opportunity of marrying into the world of the elect escape them. They were not frightened off by secret service families, in fact they would do everything to gain access to such a husband. The marriage would pay dividends for the rest of their lives.

The two ladies from records didn't have to do a thing in the factory, at most they would have English and French fashion magazines lying on their desks. They were not interested in machine specifications – nor did anyone expect them to be. The eight hours in the factory were a kind of pastime for them and it would not have occurred to anyone to ask them to translate anything. I wasn't envious of them, though; I knew that these privileges stemmed from a mixture of physical beauty, calculation and political indifference. Nor did I envy their beauty, for I knew that it was conditional, and that the conditions that enabled it were not innocent but ignominious. I only envied them their gracile shoes and elegant dresses.

The clothes, the longing for another life . . .

Socialist clothing was an absolute disgrace. There is a word in Romanian, 'ţoale': it's only used in relation to clothing and it means 'rags', but it sounds more dramatic. And this word perfectly describes the clothes of Socialism. Indigence and fear were sewn into our 'ţoale'. The clothes shops looked like rubbish dumps, the vinyl textiles smelt of loam, mud, axle grease and all sorts of chemical derivatives. Across the whole country, there were just two or three dress, skirt, blouse and jacket designs per season, all in dusty colours. They were poorly cut, lumpish and stiff, they didn't suit anyone. Whoever bought themselves something new would come across their clothes a hundred times on any street they walked down. Whenever I went into a clothes shop, I was seized by a sense of grief and repugnance. Everything looked like it smelt – and it smelt of stolen life.

At secondary school we wore dark-blue skirts and light-blue blouses, white headbands and thick, grey woollen stockings – thin, see-through stockings were prohibited. The boys dressed in dark-blue suits and light-blue shirts. The fabrics used were vulgar, greasy, matted. The worst thing about the uniform was the number which had to be sewn on to the upper arm of every item of clothing to ensure it was always visible. Every student had their own number. You weren't anonymous anywhere in the city; any passer-by could denounce you to the school principal or to the police using the number on your arm. Every morning, there was a troupe of inspectors standing at the school gates. Anyone who had attached their arm number with poppers or with just two or three stitches, rather than diligently stitching all the way round, was suspected of having pulled it off outside school, in order to be anonymous in the city. You were sent back home when something was wrong with your arm number. Then, when you came back with it correctly sewn on, you had missed a few lessons without permission. If you had several absences without permission you got a bad mark for 'conduct', which indicated insubordination. This was an important category in your school report. If you were seen as overly insubordinate you were expelled. Boys were also harassed about their hair, which had to be sufficiently short, while the girls' skirts had to be sufficiently long – down to the knee. Both were measured with a ruler at the gate in the mornings.

Could one say that the regime had a direct hold over individuals through its harassment and repression,

*but an indirect hold over everybody through the
ugliness it imposed?*

Ugliness was ubiquitous; it was the only true form of
equality under Socialism. And it was intentional, it was
part of the dictatorship's agenda. The objects produced
under Socialism ensured you grew tired of life: concrete
buildings, furniture, curtains, tableware, the flowerbeds
in the parks, posters, monuments, shop windows. As if
everything material, whether it was cement, wood, glass,
porcelain, even the branches of the trees, were in and of
itself brutal and vulgar, as if you couldn't possibly turn it
into anything more beautiful. As if, in this country, matter
sprang of its own accord into the will of the regime. This
ugly equality pressed on you, made you apathetic and unde-
manding; this was what the State wanted. For Socialism,
our heavy minds were ideal – a lust for life makes you spontaneous, and therefore unpredictable. Misery makes you
ugly. Instead of meat, the State gave us offal: pigs' feet,
which had long claws and were referred to as 'sports shoes';
or chicken feet with talons; or chicken heads in water that
had been frozen together into heavy, blue-red blocks of
ice, and which would be hacked apart into portions with
a hatchet before being weighed. People would carry the
frozen chicken heads home with their bare hands: in this
state of misery, even a handkerchief was of no use. On your
way home the ice would drip steadily, as if dogs were mark-
ing their territory with bloody urine. And everyone queued
for hours for this offal.

I think the remnants of human dignity, the most honest moments of everyday life, were the jokes: what does it
mean when your neighbour rings your doorbell? She wants

to borrow an egg. And when she knocks on the door? She's bringing back the soup bone.

Yes, I knew village grief from my childhood, and I had only *appeared* to have escaped from it. Once I had grown used to the city and saw things better, the grief returned. And the counterpart to my village grief was this methodically produced ugliness that was evenly distributed throughout the city. Socialism means the banishment of beauty.

Shortly after the fall of the Iron Curtain, I discovered the same, systematic ugliness all over Eastern Europe. Whether it was in Poland, the Czech Republic, Latvia, Slovenia, Bulgaria, in big cities or in some backwater, it was always the same. The miserable shop window displays I knew from Romania: yellowing paper napkins with hole-patterned edges laid out diagonally next to each other, so that one corner hung down vertically, and on top of them dusty bottles of fruit juice arranged in triangles; the brownish curtains on either side of the display; and endless fly shit over it all. This is the quintessential Eastern European shop window from those days – a miserable sight. It meant that I felt a little bit at home in all of these countries. How could these similarities be accidental? This Eastern European shop window is an attitude to life. It is depressive and communicates its depression day in, day out, to all those who walk past it. Even when they just happen to look at it unthinkingly, they already have this display in their mind. This shop window and the sense of home that came with it were never included in the *Landsmannschaft*'s homeland picture books.

I believe that beauty gives you something to hold on to. Ugliness makes every environment repellent; you cannot feel at home inside it. The total absence of beauty over a long period of time breeds dejection. People become defensive and ruthless. These would seem to be entirely different characteristics, but they are combined chaotically inside an individual when they have been brutalised in this way. Perhaps it is only possible to keep your balance by letting them mix erratically inside you. Similarly, you can find yourself caught up in a mixture of dissociation and rapture. Or dissociation and despair. Or rapture and despair. I believe that people's characters had long been distorted by the hopelessness they had to live in. They escalated into psychoses that escaped control and would subside as unpredictably as they had started. Every emotional state was lying in wait. I would be blindsided by my own feelings.

Earlier on in our conversation you said that the beauty of sentences gave you something to hold on to in the face of despotism. Now you are giving this a more universal resonance. Do you see a connection between our shared human need for beauty and the search for a successful sentence?

Yes. I thought in images in my day-to-day life. I drew on thought images. I had grown used to observing things in order to protect myself – from the world, but perhaps also from myself. And because it worked, it became a habit. I orientated myself facing outwards, towards the world, in order not to topple inwards and fall back into myself. It was something to keep me busy while I was walking down the street, or while I stood waiting in line. And to this day I continue to believe that the best distraction is precise observation. It's a means of dividing things up. The details grow so big that the whole disappears into them. A topic would come up by chance – for example birthmarks – and I would count them on passers-by, on their faces and necks, and the longer I paid attention to them, the more they looked like pebbles that had sprouted out of people's skin. In the same way, walking sticks became vanilla pods, and fur hats became dogs that people were wearing on their heads. Watermelons, plaster casts – I would instinctively think up an image for them, and it would stay with me. And there was a beauty to it. Aesthetics is not merely a 'stylistic device', it is substance. It shapes the things themselves, their very matter, not just the content of a sentence while writing.

The official language, which concerned itself only with slogans, must have been physically unbearable for you then?

I was appalled by the wasteland that was the Party's language. The dumbing down through platitudes – a language comprised of prefabricated parts. Sitting through the drone of work meetings, endless hours of talk, could make you feel physically sick. It was as if I had to eat everything that was said at the podium. I felt engorged, filled up with the bad taste of the words on my tongue. I couldn't swallow it any more.

But I was also continually amazed by the beauty of everyday speech – its terse, magic images. Because I sat on the staircase at the factory, I often saw the factory cats through the staircase window, even if I just happened casually to glance outside. And so I would often think of the expression: 'Every cat jumps differently at the edge of a puddle.' And for a long time, I thought that you could also say: 'Every cat jumps differently over a puddle.' But the phrasing was usually 'at the edge of', not 'over', and therefore emphasised the cat's journey to the puddle. The puddle appears unexpectedly, it takes the cat by surprise. And the cat has to hurry, so it jumps imprudently, instinct-ively, differently. I had always known the expression, but it wasn't until I was sitting on the staircase that I realised that it didn't say that the cat jumps *over* the puddle at all. 'Over' does not feature. Perhaps it jumps away from the puddle, or jumps to one side, to the right or left, or back to where it came from. It also seems to me now, when I go through all the variations, that it doesn't jump *over* the puddle because it gets startled by its own reflection.

The beauty of this expression lies in what is unsaid. It becomes a paradigm for countless moments in life. The edge of the puddle exists in everyone's life, and everyone jumps differently when presented with it. And when you hear that someone has leapt to their death, the blue sky too becomes the edge of the puddle. All the more so when the deceased is a friend. People often jumped out of the windows of tall buildings; it was the easiest way for the Securitate to frame its murders as suicides.

The unsaid unfolds like a fan inside a sentence. Under the dictatorship, the unsaid, the approximate, was everywhere, because concealment, distortion, inversion, fabrication and perversion were all familiar tools of the regime. I often only became aware of the simple, practical reality of my days through metaphors. I still cannot say how this works, but I am sure that this is how it was. The metaphors grounded me in my reality. The beauty of sentences, the indefinable, allowed for a perception so precise that I could endure the horror of what I was perceiving. This precision was not simple, or direct – it wasn't delivered to you by the literal meaning of the sentence. Instead it would form spontaneously out of a personal interaction with the words, whether gradually or suddenly.

I don't know whether one is more dependent on beauty when faced with oppression, whether one searches harder for it in private language when the official language sounds like an empty tin can and when objects are deprived of aesthetics, when the personal is quashed because the State controls everything, rubber-stamping how one can and cannot phrase things. The regime cultivated ugliness. But the language of ideology is not just hideous, it is also hostile. It destroys everything it comes across. Every one of the regime's actions was referred to using a specific phrase. Similarly, the use of a specific phrase could be tantamount to performing the action it described. The regime's use of words and its use of harassment therefore blended into each other. I believe that one listens very carefully when one knows what difference a word makes. I always listened, I searched for beauty, I waited for it to crop up. I taught myself aesthetics and then tested myself on it. This was how I calmed my nerves and tamed my fear. Having to learn your sense of aesthetics is different to inheriting one. You cannot draw on it until you have invented it. After all, without any objective criteria, it only exists in the specifics of what you have just discovered. And it must be learnt afresh with each new discovery.

You need beauty in order not to lose yourself. You need it around you, but also to see it in yourself. When I was called in to be interrogated, I would put on my make-up with particular care. This was important, it showed me that

I had not yet grown indifferent to myself. And I wanted the interrogator to see that I wasn't letting myself go. I would wear my nicest clothes. It was odd, I would spruce myself up while worrying that I might not be allowed to return home in the evening. There was a prison underneath the secret service offices – this was not just a rumour, two of my friends had already spent a week there on remand. So I would be perfectly made up and nicely dressed, but in my handbag I had a little towel, some toothpaste and my toothbrush just in case. It was all part and parcel of each interrogation. And when I was then allowed to go home again in the evening, it was as if I had been set free. I felt the paths running along beneath my feet, and the plants breathing in people's front gardens. The dahlias were the most beautiful: their petals arranged in concentric circles, forming rosettes, with a belly button in the middle. After the interrogation my head would be scrambled, my brain would be hurting. I thought my eyes were going to fall into my mouth when I closed them; my feet felt as if I had borrowed them off someone else. My journey home also felt as if it were borrowed. Until I saw the flowers, that is. The dahlias looked as though they had been waiting for me; they saw me coming and showed me how to calm myself down.

On the one hand I knew very well that the dahlias were just dahlias, that they could not see me and were not showing me anything apart from their rosettes. The dahlias were indifferent to me, but still they helped me. Because I cared about them. I felt as close to those plants on my way home from the interrogations as I had been to the plants that grew in the river valley of my childhood. They seemed to know how life worked better than I did.

Once the interrogator scared me with an unusual sentence: it was a poetic death threat. He said: whoever dresses cleanly cannot arrive in Heaven dirty. Beautiful and threatening – a sentence like that sticks with you forever.

For me, to this day, beauty has something sudden about it, something that wouldn't exist if I didn't catch it at the right moment. I don't know how to put it . . . I don't know of an aesthetics that is inherent to things, only one that is born of external and internal necessity. This is why I find it so difficult to talk about art. Ugliness didn't depend on me in the same way; it was pre-established, potent, immutable. Beauty, however, needed me in order to be beautiful. As an individual, you carried beauty around with you. It was inside you, ambulant and agitated. It was nimble and hasty, because fear is, I believe, never slow. Beauty was laced with fear; it would quicken your pulse. So too would the beauty of a sentence.

Even if you don't want to separate aesthetics in literature from aesthetics in everyday life, would you at least accept that you have a unique perspective on the world? The village girl stands before the sea and sees the biggest, flattest meadow overflowing with cuckoo flower.

It's difficult to talk about writing. You don't have to talk about it; it is of absolutely no help to your writing if you do. And I have no assurance that I am right when I say something about writing. Whatever I say about it, I need a lot of words that I wouldn't ever consider using in my writing. I find myself, when I talk about writing, in the realm of the general: I make use of categories and concepts. But these are precisely what one does not have when writing. And what I do have when I am writing is not available to me outside the writing process. I cannot speak the way I write. It would be foolhardy to try.

You also connect writing to silence – in both cases, one has to work out what one is carrying around. The belief that we can get the better of chaos by talking, you say, is something that you have only come across in the West.

Yes, writing has to do with silence, not with speech. The sentences say something, of course, but it is something that you have worked out for yourself, in the privacy of your own mind – you were complicit with silence, not with speech. I would never have said to anyone that the sea was a vast meadow or that the spume was cuckoo flower. Nor would I have said it to myself either. Well, all right, I might have thought it to myself, but what of it . . . It wouldn't have been anything special. It would just have happened, fleetingly; I wouldn't have noticed it. But everything changes when I write it down. Then I don't have to say it with my mouth. If I write the words down, they are able to say something which I would feel embarrassed about had I said it out loud.

My childhood taught me how to remain silent while in company. We would work together in the fields in silence, or sit silently together round the dining table. As a child, I was told that you shouldn't talk during meals. People spoke more in the city, and for the first time I met people who spoke about themselves, even if you barely knew them. It was not unusual for someone to tell you on the tram about their illness, or about what they were keen to buy or were planning to cook for dinner. These monologues served no purpose; this was talking as a means to relieve oneself. When I arrived in Germany, I was surprised at how seldom someone would strike up a conversation on the train. People kept an eye on each other, but they didn't want the other person to notice. When confined in a train compartment, you can feel these looks sizing you up.

People in the West speak with purpose. These days, many people use the word 'communicating', which sounds to me as if you were on stage or at a convention. It's suggestive of preprogrammed speech. Here in Germany, many people believe that talking always helps and that you should talk about everything. People say that as long as we speak to each other there'll be no wars. I don't believe this. Talking can antagonise and agitate. Words can appease conflicts, but they can ignite them too. And things ignite quickly; the way states interact is no different to the relationship between individuals. There are conflicts on both a personal and national scale that one cannot talk one's way out of – and nor might one want to. There are positions, principles and values which one cannot forgo.

What is done determines what is said. And the reverse is just as true. And, taken together, these deeds and words determine what is achieved – whether you destroy or preserve. But can one tell the direction of travel beforehand? And are the motivations clear after the fact? After all, there are always many ways of being guilty and just as many ways one might be in the right. Dictatorships rely on people being overwhelmed by fabricated guilt, while making it clear that an individual can never be in the right – that privilege is reserved for the State.

When I am thinking about something, a discussion takes place inside my head that has no need of words. That is, the way I talk to myself is completely different to the way that words speak. I cannot at all express in words what I think to myself. Seen from outside, it is nothing but silence.

I have never been able to believe that talking will set the world to rights, because I knew it on a personal level: however much I spoke to somebody, the things I was up against would not change. All right, talking has a better chance when you are not living under a dictatorship – at least talk is left to its own devices then and not constantly instrumentalised. Under a dictatorship, two-thirds of life is impossible, absolutely nothing is up to you and you can't change this. And the final third – that which is private – is beset by harassment. Intimacy tries to save itself, but the filth of politics infiltrates your relationships and makes you pay a heavy cost for your friendships. Love collapses; your nerves go haywire. How often we all experienced this . . .

After all, an interrogation is also about talking – it's more or less exclusively about talking. But whom was I talking to? The fellow behind the desk wore two shoes, just like I did, but he was not a person; he was an instrument, a regime, the State itself. He decided what I spoke about, when I spoke about it and for how long.

Being interrogated means *having* to talk, that's one thing. The other is having no choice about whom you're speaking to. In my daily life, there were a lot of people I didn't want to talk to at all. I despised them. They were responsible for terrible things, they lived sordid lives, behaved brutishly or subserviently, and I wanted nothing to do with them. I wouldn't have been able to bring myself to talk to them. Nor did they talk to me.

Freedom makes people thoughtless. But this is also a piece of good fortune. There is no adversary you have to constantly assert yourself against – whether actively or latently. In a totalitarian world, a hundred things are constantly happening to you. And you are constantly on your toes. You have to switch your brain on, think, understand it all, draw conclusions, react. You have to react immediately, dive into an alternative way of being. You decide in the moment, based on an internal image of yourself. You know what you expect of yourself.

If I had allowed my fear to push me into agreeing to the Securitate's recruitment offer in the factory, I would have been a different person from that moment on – a person at war with myself. My internal image would have punished me for that decision. How else can I explain it? I would no longer have been able to get along with myself. I would have reproached myself to such an extent that it would have been difficult to bear. There was no courage involved at all; it was a necessary decision.

The same goes for when you're writing. You weigh up speaking and staying silent, and both remain tangled up in each other. Allusion and omission – it's all one big labyrinth. More than through their content, it is through rhythm and sound that words establish their necessity. And finding the right way to put these words together is at once fascinating and tedious. Often, I am no match for this condition. There are times when my nerves can't handle writing. Then I can't work at all. I can't put myself through having to endure what the sentences decide. But I have never viewed this as a crisis. On the contrary, it's something of a relief to remove the act of writing from my life for as long as possible.

Your use of language is strongly influenced by Romanian, which you describe as 'sensual, impudent and surprisingly beautiful'. You don't actually write in Romanian, but it is constantly looking over your shoulder.

Yes, when I write, the Romanian language writes with me. That I learnt it so late certainly played a big part in shaping my relationship with the language. There were no Romanians in the village, and school was conducted in German. Romanian was taught around three times a week as a foreign language, and apart from during these lessons no one spoke Romanian. I was fifteen years old when I arrived in the city. My secondary school was also in German, but everywhere outside lessons people spoke only Romanian. The streets, the shops, the government agencies, the passers-by – the whole city spoke Romanian. I spoke as little as possible and listened, as much as I could, to the words. The soft diphthongs and triphthongs such as *'toate'* – all – and *'oaie'* – sheep – you didn't get those in German. I so liked saying the words out loud; they felt so beautiful in your mouth. From the very beginning – how can I put it? – they tasted good, aesthetically. If only for the practical reason of getting my bearings, I felt a keen desire to learn the language. In your daily life in the city, you were wrapped up in Romanian. And the longer I listened to the language, the more I liked the metaphors, the long dramatic expletives, the many nuances of diminutives, from the cynical to the sentimental. Not to mention the sayings and the superstition.

When a star falls, German people are supposed to make a wish, while Romanians say someone has died. Or take the pheasant, for instance: it is a bird that can't fly very well, it gets ensnarled in the undergrowth and is easy prey. All of this is contained in the Romanian expression: 'Man is a great pheasant in the world.' Man, too, is easy prey: he can't assert himself, he overpays, he is no match for life. However, in German the pheasant is a braggart. The German language has made a saying out of the bird's appearance, while the Romanian saying is based on its character. I feel closer to the sad Romanian pheasant. This is why one of my books is titled *Man is a Great Pheasant in the World.**

I felt like this about the names of plants, too. Lilies of the valley, or May bells, are called 'little teardrops' in Romanian. And yes, when I look at the flower, its blossom is strung just like teardrops rolling down a cheek. Somehow 'teardrops' are more beautiful than 'bells'. I learnt that in Romanian a birthmark is called a 'little hazelnut'. And the word *'minte'* means both 'intelligence' and 'lying'. Shoelace, *'şiret'*, also means clever. And *'coasta'* means both coast and rib. Or take the sayings: 'rubbing mint' means 'wasting time'. There were always comparisons to be had. My mother tongue and my national tongue watched each other as I learnt this new language. I am referring only to the spoken language that belonged to the people, of course, not the concrete-covered, grey State language. That was unbearable.

It often turned out that the Romanian language was better suited to my disposition, that its attitude to life was a better fit for me. There was also the Swabian dialect that

---

* Published in the English translation as *The Passport* (London: Serpent's Tail, 1989).

stood between them, my village German. It was this gaze, the understanding borne through this language, that was displaced by the Romanian – luckily. It took years, but at some point Romanian was so familiar to me that it was as if my surroundings had learnt the language for me, or as if the language had nestled up against me. I had arrived inside the language: I no longer thought in German when I spoke Romanian.

These days, this is no longer the case, unfortunately. Over the past twenty years I have seldom spoken Romanian, and I am losing many of my words. I have to cling to what comes to mind and speak between the gaps. It's a shame. My Swabian dialect, on the other hand, my very first language, remains, no matter how long I don't speak it for. It's buried in my skull, and to this day I have not forgotten a single word. I'd like to swap: to keep the Romanian and forget the dialect. But how? However much I liked it, Romanian never became my mother tongue. I would never have been able to write in Romanian. I was missing the crucial element required for me to do so, though I don't know what that is.

But words are of course not just letters, they place an image in your head. You can forget the words, because the images have grown inside you, and they remain. The German word '*Maiglöckchen*', 'May bells' or 'lily of the valley', also contains the image of the Romanian word. I will see little teardrops on the plant for all time; the image does not depend on the word itself. However many words I lose, Romanian still writes with me.

And with this different gaze came a different tone,
a different rhythm, a different rhyme. Particularly

*in music – the songs had a different grammar
of feeling . . .*

I came to music through the Romanian language. I knew rock musicians. They wanted to know what was going on musically in other countries, and so they would get hold of records just as we got hold of books. They worked a lot with authentic folklore when they were composing. Romanian folklore is sublime. Maria Tănase* is just one example, there are also the old men's choirs – they give you goosebumps. And there is the basic structure of the *'doina'*, a traditional type of song in Romania which is categorised according to different emotional states: the *doina* of suffering, the *doina* of joy. From birth to death, there are songs for every moment of one's life, and they are all poetic, not clichés. When someone sings 'I want to drink your eyes out of a glass made of quartz', where are we? We are in the realm of lyricism, the most beautiful lyricism. I knew German folk music in the village, it was all brass band music, and stiffly tramping about to a polka. It meant nothing to me as a child; it didn't speak to my feet or to my mind.

Well, all right, just as there was the State language, Romania also had its share of folklore fabricated by the State. It was ungainly and empty. The poetic, authentic folk music was banned from the State media, because the roots of its emotion – joy or suffering – were in the individual, in human beings. The regime couldn't tolerate such stuff. Real

---

*   Maria Tănase (1913–63) was a Romanian singer and actress who drew heavily on traditional Romanian folk music. She is one of Romania's major icons of the twentieth century; the country's equivalent to France's Édith Piaf.

folklore was subversive because of its authenticity. This is why the State cultivated its own ideological folklore. It was Socialist folklore: pop songs full of praise for the Party, and stirring anthems sung by choirs of workers. This Party kitsch tootled out of the telly, and musicians would scrape their fiddles, regurgitating it all around the country at State festivals and for national holidays. And it blared out of the loudspeakers in the factory courtyard every morning and during our lunch breaks. In the dark of the early morning, the loudspeakers tortured us with stomping melodies and mendacious lyrics. The songs pressed on your skull; the factory courtyard would lurch and I would stumble across the yard as if the cobbles were kicking at the backs of my knees.

And during meals, whether you liked it or not, you would be chewing in rhythm with the music. I knew who selected our daily music: one of the four accountants from my previous office. He was an old Hungarian Communist and he was the first to arrive at the factory in the morning. He had his own separate box room, like a rabbit hutch. We all ate in the office, but he would eat in his hutch, sitting among his magnetic tapes. He had kidney stones, and would often be sitting there in obvious agony, with a grey-green face. And he was masochistic: even on these days he wouldn't neglect the music.

Romanians have always had an intimate relationship with music. Whenever they come together somewhere, songs immediately spring into being. People sang on the site of the revolution in 1989; the songs are haunting, both the music itself and the lyrics.

National Socialism ruined so much for us Germans; we can no longer establish a connection of this kind. When something has been torn to pieces, it can't be made whole again. German folklore has no role to play in daily life. There is just a hole, a deep emptiness. In order to sing, you need it to be a matter of course. We stand on the other side now, but our songs stand back over there, where they were bawled out by Hitler, serving as the soundtrack to war and crime. I couldn't bear my father's songs. When he sang *'Schwarzbraun ist die Haselnuss'* ['Black-brown is the hazelnut'], black-brown took on an entirely different meaning. Germany, the land of poets and thinkers – what a narcissistic, laughable idea.

Yes, the Romanians were fascists too, and they deny their crimes to this day. And yes, they have *two* dictator-ships to their name. But their folklore is so intractable, so radical in its poetry, that it was ill-suited to these dic-tatorships. It resisted the process of *'Gleichschaltung'*, it couldn't be brought into line, neither under fascism nor Socialism; it had to be banned. It was cast aside by the State, but listened to in secret. The ban made the folk-loric private and intimate. You carry songs in your head, you whistle them, you hum them, you mouth the words to yourself silently. I know it from the factory: people had their songs. I too would hum along in time with my steps on my way to an interrogation. I was so afraid of getting there and yet I had to go. Such a song in your head was a hiding place – a beautiful, portable hiding place.

How much were you shaped by the language of your childhood? There are so many snippets of dialogue or turns of phrase that you draw on which are literary, full of dark humour, surprising, that perfectly hit

their mark. Just as an example, your grandfather
once said: 'When the flags start to flutter, people's
brains slip into their trumpets.'

What is 'the literary'? What's literary is of course not something unique to writing; it can crop up anywhere. It appears at every turn, in folklore, in proverbs and figures of speech, in the images of superstition. Every language is full of metaphors. How else do compound words such as *'Augapfel'* [literally 'eye apple', meaning 'eyeball'], *'Landzunge'* ['tongue of land' or 'headland'] and *'muttersee-lenallein'* [literally 'mother-soul-alone', meaning 'all alone'] come into being. The poetic was not invented by writers, after all. I imagine that every one of our metaphors was once said accidentally or intentionally by someone. And someone else adopted it, used it countless times, until it slowly came to be accepted. There are thousands of metaphors, which we use out of habit, without paying any heed to the fact that they are poetic.

My grandfather had picked up this sentence somewhere, or he may even have thought it up himself. This doesn't mean that my grandfather was profoundly poetic. 'Don't think where you shouldn't,' a sentence my grandmother frequently used, is also poetic. That's why it is engraved in my memory. You don't need to know the word 'poetry' to have a sense of poetic urgency. Back then, as a child, I didn't even know that literature existed, but this sentence churned me up.

It's such an incisive image, too. The context is that your
uncle was turned into a passionate National Socialist
in school — there could scarcely be a sharper description

*of the obliteration of one's own thought in the
roar of propaganda.*

When my grandfather spoke of the fluttering flags and
people's brains slipping into their trumpets, he did so in
High German, not in dialect. Perhaps he was quoting the
sentence, or perhaps he formulated it in High German in
order to elevate it. He fought in the First World War, his
son in the Second. The sentence is about subservience and
fanaticism – both applied to his dead son.

My uncle had fallen in the war, but he was always there
in the house. He was a phantom. The penultimate photograph taken of him hung on the wall. My grandfather had
blacked out the runes on his Nazi uniform using burnt
match ends, but they still shimmered through. And in a
drawer, inside my grandmother's prayer book, was the last
picture of him, it was just a little bigger than a match-
box. It had been sent from the front. A white sheet on an
empty field and in the middle of the sheet lay something
dark – this was her son, torn to shreds by a mine. I would
sometimes go to the drawer and secretly take a look at the
picture. It fascinated me and made my flesh creep that the
dark stain on the white sheet was my dead uncle.

And in the other room stood his accordion. And the
Encyclopaedia and the Doctor Book had also been his, left
over from his library. He had been apprenticed to a trades-
man for a while and was turned into a fervent Nazi there.
He played chief ideologue in the village, gave speeches,
denounced people who didn't want to sign up for the war.
As a soldier, he had been appointed to an administrative
position in the Romanian army, but he wanted to fight for
Hitler and volunteered for the SS.

My grandmother would tell us about his library. That after the war, the Russians came into the village, went from house to house and spread terror. That she, as a woman, had stayed in the house all on her own, because my grandfather was interned in a camp at the other end of the country as an 'exploiter of the people', while my mother had been deported to a forced labour camp in Russia. Part of his library must have consisted of Hitler books, said my grandmother, but which ones were they? She had had no time to sort through them, it would have taken days. Nor would she have known with certainty whether a particular book was harmless or dangerous. The Russians were cruel and merciless, she said, you're not going to let yourself be shot because of books. She burnt all the books, one after the other, in her oven out of fear.

It was a brick oven, the rear of which jutted out in the corner of the kitchen, while the door was in an adjacent pantry. We used it to heat the house with big bundles of cornstalks. You could sit round the oven wall and warm your back. You could even climb on to it. It was as wide as a double bed; three people could sleep on top of it. We would bake bread inside it every week.

The photo on the wall, the photo in the prayer book, the oven, the Encyclopaedia, the Doctor Book – they were all connected to my dead uncle. As was the terrible accordion. Its case was covered with a white sheet, much like my uncle was in the image from the front that was kept in the prayer book. The accordion stood in the darkest room, the one we went into least. And when I stepped into the room, the white sheet would glow like an altar. The accordion was a relic.

But then my mother decided I should learn to play

it. I had to go to an accordion lesson twice a week. The teacher was as old as my grandfather and was called Wastl. He lived far away; I would carry the accordion on my back through the village. When I arrived at his house, his cane was already lying on the table. When I pressed the wrong key, he would hit me on the fingers. The more often he hit me, the more often I would press the wrong key. I would play *'Muss I denn zum Städtele hinaus'* ['Must I then to the Village'], *'Kornblumenblau'* ['Cornflower Blue'] or *'O wie wohl ist mir am Abend'* ['Oh how lovely is the Evening'],* and I would make mistakes and weep as I did so. He would say I had to stay sitting there and practise until I could play them without making any mistakes. He would leave me to do so on my own, and I would see him working in the garden. He would stay outside for two, three hours. Or he'd come in from time to time to take a look and check whether I was practising, and then disappear again. I would sit there, fused to this accordion. I would squeak out these songs or just stare into space and listen to the ticking of the clock instead of practising. I had to find a way of getting myself out of this, somehow – I started to wind the clock forward, to make time pass more quickly. I started by moving the hands on ten minutes, but since this didn't work I kept having to help it along a little bit more. I thought that one day he would believe the clock and let me leave.

Of course, he noticed that the clock always ran fast when I had my accordion lesson. And he took revenge for it. He left a crumpled bank note under the table. And I

---

* Traditional Swabian and German folk songs. The first was performed by Elvis Presley in an English adaptation entitled 'Wooden Heart', during his days as a GI.

thought that if someone had lost the money, then I could take it. I had found it after all, even if it wasn't lying in the street. Ten lei, it was enough to buy a good number of sweets. I picked up the note, smoothed it out, folded it up small and tucked it into my stocking. And then I was hit with shock at what I had done. No – I was shocked by the ticking of the clock. I desperately wanted to keep the money, but instead I pulled it out of my stocking after all and crumpled it up again and put it back under the table. Which was lucky, because when my mother paid him his monthly fee for the accordion lessons, Wastl said that while I fiddled with the clock, at least I didn't steal.

I can't remember how long I had to learn the accordion for. It must have been over a year. Because I remember the winter days when old Wastl couldn't go out to the garden and would hammer around in a workshop at the back of the house instead when he left me on my own. Yes, it was the second spring when, on my way home past the well, I decided to put an end to my accordion lessons. The well was in the middle of the village; it was the only one on the way home. Night was falling, but it wasn't dark yet. The ice was sparkling on the sides of the well. It had a big wheel, and a chain with two buckets wound round a wooden spool. They moved synchronously: the empty bucket went down, while the full one came up out of the depths. I put the accordion into the empty bucket and lashed its strap to the chain with my handkerchief. Then I let the bucket down into the dark well and listened to how the accordion clapped against the water. Suddenly a dog barked next to me. Don't think I didn't see that, a woman cried, but she was too late, the accordion had already taken its bath. She pulled up the bucket and carried it, dripping, to my home.

And I followed her – I wasn't even afraid, I trotted home like a pet, where else was I supposed to go.

That evening was awful. I was beaten with a broom – I ran round the table and my mother even threw the chairs at me. And my grandmother was sobbing as if her son had died a second time. My grandfather put the accordion into the oven to dry out.

After a few days it had dried, but its pleats remained puffy and developed cracks and its keys would jump out of place. The accordion was dead. It was packed into its case in the dark room.

What I had done to the accordion, and thus to my dead uncle, was so monstrous that no one could speak about it, even the next day. No one wanted to think about it ever again. So I was only punished for it on that one day, and I never had to play the accordion again.

A Man with a Bouquet

*The Land of Green Plums tells the story of a group
of friends who find themselves in the sights of the
secret service after they refuse to accept the official story
that one of their classmates died by suicide. Instead,
they start to ask questions and investigate what really
happened. One of the absurdities is that Lola, the
student who has committed suicide, is expelled
from the Party during a meeting.*

This was the reality. When I was a student, another student was posthumously expelled from the Party. She had hanged herself with a belt inside her closet. The whole hall of residence was in turmoil, everyone was talking about it. Suicide was a public taboo. I think her expulsion from the Party was a 'preventive' measure, as strange as it was to do this *after* her death. The act of throwing her out of the Party was supposed to avoid such a thing ever happening again in their halls of residence. For the university, the location of her suicide was unbearable. Such a commotion was a danger to everyday life; you needed calm and obedience. A suicide in the halls of residence, with six to eight girls in every room and one closet between them all, was perceived as an anti-Socialist act because you couldn't hush it up. A big post-mortem meeting was organised in order to portray the suicide as an affront to the university and to the Party. They said the dead girl 'did not deserve' to be a student at 'our' university and a member of 'our' Party. The misfortune of the deceased, her hopelessness, were exhibited as treason. The hijacking of the students by including them in this constant use of 'our' was shameless enough. But the most abhorrent thing about this event was the utter lack of humanity. The girl who had hanged herself no longer belonged to the university or to the Party anyway; she had left them of her own accord, through her death. The real message of this meeting was: if you kill yourselves, find a different place to do it, don't bother us with your corpse.

Over the following weeks, a fragile sky hung over the halls of residence, and an unreal silence settled around the concrete blocks of the university and in the scrub of the park. It seemed to me as if none of us were standing on secure ground. We would walk, and step through our own foreheads as we walked. We were barefoot in the face.

Many years later, in my days of defamation at the factory, I too considered suicide. I searched for the right place – the window at the top of my block of flats – or the right stones for my coat pocket and the right spot along the river. But then the 'blond visitor' at the factory banished any thought of suicide. He threatened me by saying, we'll throw you in the river. My suicide would have been a gift for the scumbag. So with that it was over, I became hungry for life. During the worst of the harassment, I had forgotten how to sleep. I was so chronically tired that the wind blew right through me. My feet were made of lead and my head was a glass sphere, transparent. I know what being in such a state is like. 'Barefoot in the face' is not a surreal image, but rather the only one that describes this state.

As I have mentioned, I always clung to plants, and I continue to do so to this day. They reveal what cannot be said with words. After the post-mortem meeting at the university, even the blossoming lime trees had become intertwined with the suicide. They were half-withered, and strewed yellow dust on to the paths, fences and roofs. Everything was bright and smelt as only large amounts of half-withered lime trees can smell – everything smelt of corpse sugar. I don't know why, but once there is a colour attached to a difficult thing you have experienced, it will come back to you when something similar happens. When, years later, I considered suicide myself, everything was bright again.

This is how I came to the conclusion that suicide in the city is bright, that it shines through milky-white.

But I knew suicide already, from the village, and there it struck me as dark, as indigo-blue. The colour had something to do with mulberries. My aunt's father had hanged himself from the mulberry tree in the courtyard out back. He would often play with me, and I adored him. He had a stuffed owl that sat on a branch on the wall in his room. He slept in this room and was not afraid of the owl – but we were all afraid, because owls called Death into the house when they settled on the roof. The stuffed owl could no longer hoot, but it remained an owl. A white owl – a barn owl – not a death owl, said my aunt. I didn't entirely believe this argument. After all, the dead were given a white shroud in their coffin. And her father hanged himself years later in the mulberry tree, from a branch just like the one his white owl sat on. His suicide was dark, with an indigo-blue hoop round his neck.

In the city, the act of 'suicide' was often taken out of your hands – and those who were responsible did their dirty work and never recoiled in horror at their actions, no matter how brightly they were illuminated.

The way the regime dealt with suicide was perverse. On the one hand it couldn't ever be mentioned in public, and yet at the same time deaths were staged as suicides in order to cover up political murders.

So the elite claimed for itself the authority to interpret death: it represented murder as suicide and suicide as an accident?

If it was a traffic collision, poisoning, defenestration, drowning or hanging, then the doctor would come and write 'suicide' on the death certificate. Although it was required by law, an autopsy was denied in such cases.

It was like that with my friend Roland Kirsch,* too. He lived alone, and was found by his mother hanging in his flat. The neighbours had heard loud voices the night before, yet to this day it says 'suicide' on his death certificate. They were denied an autopsy, the police 'helped' his parents to collect all the necessary papers, and he was swiftly put in the ground. There were more than enough secret service doctors who would write whatever the authorities needed on the certificates, and hospitals were at the disposal of the secret service too.

---

*   Roland Kirsch (1960–89) was a Romanian writer of Banat Swabian origin and was involved with the *Aktionsgruppe Banat*.

Suicide was even more taboo when Party bigwigs took their own lives. Following the example set by our dictator, provincial leaders would go hunting. Barely anyone else had a hunting licence, it was a privilege, a sign of trust on the part of the regime. So if a Party official died by suicide, the papers would say that a faithful comrade had died in a tragic hunting accident. Nobody believed the papers, because rumour would have it that he had shot himself in the mouth. But it was impossible to conceal the death of a Party cadre who was famous throughout the city, and since suicide, especially for someone in their position, was humiliatingly at odds with the supposed happiness of the Romanian people under Ceauşescu, the Party saved face by calling it an accident, even if nobody believed it. For the Party, the point wasn't to be believed; the point was obedience, and for them to profit from their position of power.

On the subject of suicide as taboo, I always think of Paul Celan, and how you can lie more with a half-truth than if you were to completely obfuscate the facts. Our schoolbook, as it did with all of its texts, included the author's biography alongside his famous poem 'Death Fugue'. But it did not mention that, beset by guilt after surviving the camps, Celan died by suicide in the Seine. Suicide was taboo, and the biographies had to set a positive example, especially when it came to great writers. And Romania's fascist past was also taboo, as was the fact that the concentration camps in Transnistria were under Romanian administration. There was to be no word about the fact that racial laws, like those of the Nazis, had applied in Romania during the same period. Ghettos, pogroms, concentration camps – the Romanians carried out their work conscientiously and were praised by the Nazis. Romanian fascism had its own billowing language: sickly-sweet, religious-national. The Orthodox Church was firmly integrated into fascism. Death was, admittedly, 'a master from Germany', but it had an assiduous apprentice from Romania. To this day, this is a fact that is kept quiet.

One must beware half-truths. They shouldn't have included 'Death Fugue' in the schoolbook, but they needed it in order to pin their own crimes on the Nazis. They didn't need to deny anything, they just needed to suppress a few key details. The misrepresentation of history was intentional. This way, the lie was not fully articulated, but it was still spread. And they would have been able to fend off the accusation of misrepresentation – after all, no one had lied directly. I am quite certain that the Ministry of Education will have carefully planned its misuse of 'Death Fugue'.

Let us return, briefly, to the dead student's expulsion from the Party. Everybody in the auditorium voted in favour of this decision. Lola herself would have raised her hand too, you write, but that didn't count any more. Doesn't this show how the individual participates in conditions that will later destroy them?

What does 'conditions that will destroy them' mean? Most people would not describe this as destruction. If you want to make something of yourself in a dictatorship, you have to conform. And most people do want to make something of themselves: they want a secure job and a salary. Even remaining inconspicuous is only possible at the price of keeping quiet – and you haven't actually made anything of yourself if you only go unnoticed. So you have to at least pretend that you are conforming. In a dictatorship, the destruction of the individual is normal, it is unavoidable. Either you are destroyed by conforming to the regime, or you are destroyed through non-compliance. I viewed striving to advance your career within the strictures of Ceaușescu's regime as a form of destruction which the person had consented to. One's only choice was between destruction through consent or self-destruction through non-compliance. Over the years, I would notice more and more how thin my nerves were growing. I felt broken, no longer intact. The approach I had taken as a student was to stay in the grey area between conforming to the system and openly opposing it. I missed classes as often as possible; I studied as little as possible; I read books that were forbidden at university. I didn't attach any value to good marks, but I did manage to slip through the exams.

I didn't attend the post-mortem meeting, even though our presence was mandatory, not because I was being brave but because I felt such revulsion towards the whole affair. I wouldn't have been able to bear it. The girls from our hall of residence told me about the frenetic applause. Perhaps people were clapping with dread, but this didn't throw them off-rhythm. All day, the officials said 'one must' or 'we must'. Many people were used to this 'must', they had learnt to function without thinking about what they were doing. It had been drilled into them, almost all of their sentences started with this 'must'. And one 'must' always be present at university. Being seen to be present was more important than anything else. One of the main purposes of university was control. Being present at all lectures, writing down every word and unthinkingly parroting it all back verbatim at the exams – that was what got you the best marks. This was the path of least resistance. I think most people didn't actually want to have any thoughts of their own.

There was a utility room on each floor of our halls of residence in which we could dry our laundry. It also contained an iron and ironing board, and a shared fridge for food. Aside from the usual things like salami and cheese, there would also be raw liver, bloody kidneys and pig or calf hearts in our fridge, sometimes even a plate with a brain on it. In a side street very close to the halls of residence was an abattoir. I never knew whom this offal belonged to, and where and how you could cook it. We had no stove, after all. When you went to the fridge late at night, the offal was already blue and the blood had dried black. And because the light from the bulb inside the fridge was so shockingly white, the offal seemed to gaze back at you with a very different look to the one it had during the daytime. Sometimes I would imagine that the offal belonged to my fellow students, particularly the hearts; that they would remove them from their own body in the evening and put them in the fridge, in order to sleep better. Standing before this fridge full of offal, I said the words 'heart-beast'* to myself in my head for the first time. This word had the same effect as the sight of the cold entrails in the fridge. Just as how the phrase 'corpse sugar' had the same effect as the half-withered lime trees in the city.

I didn't know the student who had hanged herself. The word back then was that she had worked for the secret service. At the time, I simply believed it. This was before I learnt through my own bitter experience how the Securitate

---

* *Herztier*, or 'heart-beast', is the original title of *The Land of Green Plums*.

operated. All I knew then was that it existed. But later on, I could well imagine how the Securitate could drive anybody, even one of their informers, to suicide.

The informers were privileged, of course, but not unconditionally so. They had signed a contract after all, they had taken an oath of collaboration. They had offered up their privacy to the State; they had to practise perfidy, learn how to influence without attracting attention, and how to act deviously and appear harmless in order to carry out their orders. I do not feel sorry for the informers, but it really was a skulking, miserable life – unless the informing brought them satisfaction and a feeling of power, of course. Once they had signed up, they only appeared to be the same person as before; suddenly they had two faces when they looked at themselves in the mirror. And something could always go wrong. Any slip-up in an informer's behaviour could betray them and wreak havoc, rendering entire strategies ineffective.

During the time of the great harassment, I remained thankful every day that I was free, albeit at my own peril. Unlike the informers, I did not have to see two faces looking back at me in the mirror. And, most important of all: I didn't have to stab anybody in the back.

It may well be the case, indeed it is probable, that the student, if she was an informer, was driven to her death by the secret service – that she was threatened with being thrown out of the university or with time in prison or with death.

We know now from the files that not all informers were safe. If an informer really disappointed the secret service, or if they no longer wanted to continue, the State did not simply let them go, they let them fall. They were seen as a traitor. And they'd seek revenge; the whole relationship was upended. In many cases, treason was punished just as severely as non-compliance.

> *If you are not safe, even as an informer, does this mean that fear has everyone in its grip: those who do not comply, of course, but also those who do join in? Are the only exceptions the demented — those who, as you have written, had exchanged fear for insanity?*

One cannot exchange fear for insanity. A person's insanity does not ease their fear; it is added on top of it. A friend once took me with him to a psychiatric hospital. He was a rock musician and had worked there for a while as a music therapist. A doctor had offered him the job so that he could earn a bit of money, because his band wasn't allowed to give any concerts. There weren't any other music therapists anywhere in the country; it was a personal experiment of the doctor's. Perhaps the rock musician managed to get people to sing or dance, released them from their tristesse for a moment each day, who knows.

The hospital stood behind vast cereal fields, there was nothing else there otherwise. The poppies were blooming. There were shrubs and long grass in the hospital courtyard, and poplars enclosed the site. The trees were black with crows' nests, and the cawing was so loud — as if the crows knew what was going on inside the lunatics' minds. The doctor showed me a few patients who had been driven mad by political persecution. He also said that most of the 'politicals' had been abandoned by their own families, that they were now alone in the world, that no one ever visited them. Insanity forgets nothing, and so they were still being tortured by their persecutors, the doctor said. You might think, he continued, that if you reach a state of insanity you enter into a different reality, and forget whatever has driven you to madness – but this is not the case. Your fears continue to churn in your mind. If you listen to what the patients are saying, each one will reveal to you why they have ended up in this madhouse.

During my visit, I learnt that we always suffer because of who we are, even when we lose track of who that person is. It had always seemed to me that the city's lunatics had agreed to take on the burden of what we all lived under – and that in so doing, they relieved the supposedly sane people of their bad consciences.

The man who stands on the street every day with a bow tie round his neck and brittle flowers in his hand, waiting for his wife, who is supposedly about to be released from prison. The 'philosopher' who mistakes tree trunks and pylons for people. The dwarf lady with shaggy hair who stands by the monument. All of these people live in public, entirely without protection.

Well, all of us had our own psychoses. Inside people's heads, everything looked like the Socialist clothes shops or the homeland shop windows. It was all temporary, everything was temporary. Things didn't get better – but they could get worse. In the city there were lunatics who belonged to the place where they stood. Or the other way round: the place belonged to them, they infused it with an aura, a dark sensibility. Passers-by would only look at them fleetingly, but I think everyone had their own thoughts about them; you couldn't pass by them without feeling some kind of emotion. They were the background artists of all our lives. I didn't know the man with the bouquet personally, but he really did stand for years on the Corso in Timişoara, and people always said he was waiting for his wife. And there was the dwarf lady on the square with the monument, who looked almost like a stray animal. She too had been living there for years, had settled outside in the open. That the worst never happened to her, even in our brutalised country, was something of a miracle. The lunatics of the city made themselves invulnerable: because they were lacking any protection, even the most unscrupulous thugs treated them with awe and respect. They were almost common property; we had to look after them. It was an unwritten law, even for the police, that one should not assault them, humiliate them or ridicule them. There were religious fears involved too: that you would be punished by God and go mad yourself if you treated them badly.

With everyone else the police were brutal, meting out blows and kicks, cudgelling people. The police were mostly very young, half-illiterate. Ambitious and well trained, they carried out any dirty work for the regime. But they came from tiny, remote villages, and underneath their uniforms they still nursed the superstition of the poor.

The man with the bouquet didn't live on the street like the dwarf lady, he came and went. He was dressed perfectly every day, would look down the street and hold his bouquet upright in front of his chest. Yes, and down the street was the prison. People said he was waiting for his wife. The wife had died long ago, but she had been locked up in the prison towards the end of her life. Had he seen her there? Had he gone with her? People told him that if she was alive and were released, she would come out on to this street and walk straight up to him. Nobody knew why she had been sent to prison. I think people didn't actually want to know; specific reasons might have disturbed the general sentimentality. Presumably the reasons were not political, or the man would not have been able to wait for years undisturbed. The contrast – that someone could be neat and smartly dressed, could still appear to have things in hand, and yet be crazy, that they could stand there with a bouquet while being in an entirely different reality – this was as awe-inspiring as it was incomprehensible. And for all those years, people thought this man was living in an eternal love story. It's quite possible that the Securitate psychologists had realised that having the lunatics in the city centre was conducive to political stability. They inspired compassion and gentleness, and thus inhibited aggression. Plus, if the thousands of passers-by were to compare themselves to the dwarf lady as they walked past her, they would all feel content with their own lives.

Whenever I saw the man with the bouquet, I thought of Veronika with her guinea fowl. She, thank God, had not lost her mind, but she was waiting for her husband in her remote village just as vainly as this man was waiting for his wife in the centre of the city. She didn't need a bouquet, because she had the wind at the alley gate. And you simply can't carry that in your hands.

You said that the worst never befell the dwarf lady. But something does happen to her, at least in the novel: she is raped repeatedly. And because she is deaf and unable to speak, she does not hear the arrival of the men, and she cannot scream when they assault her.

No character is a carbon copy, not in any novel. Yes, the dwarf lady was deaf. She was young and she would occasionally have a belly which would then disappear, as if she had had an abortion. I know nothing about her, neither who she was nor where she came from. She was bedraggled. Unlike the man with the bouquet, she lived on the street. And when she was pregnant, I am sure no one asked her whether she wanted to bring a child into the world or not. She probably wouldn't even have been able to decide this for herself anyway. Nor would anybody have trusted her to make that decision. What was she supposed to do with a newborn out in the open in the summer heat and the dust, or in the biting frost and knee-deep snow? The State would have had to take her off the street and into its 'custody'. And nobody would have wished that upon her . . . She would have been locked away, and the child would have been sent to one of those gruesome orphanages. Whichever direction you thought in, her fate was tragic, and she remained feeble-minded and deaf, unable to speak and *mutterseelen-allein* – all alone. There could be no happy end for her.

Many women came to a tragic end when they got pregnant in Romania. Ceaușescu had issued a decree that required every woman to bear five children. But there wasn't enough of even the most basic foodstuffs in the country. And even if there had been sufficient supplies for everyone, there was hardly a single Romanian family that would have wanted to have five children of their own free will. Abortions were prohibited; they landed you in prison. There was no contraception. Thousands of families were destroyed by this decree.

Women could only have abortions illegally, and so they ended up in unsafe hands – who, more often than not, would botch it. Many women died. Others developed complications, and they had to go to hospital. There, their first visitor was the secret service, and it was only once they were prepared to betray the botcher that the doctor would help them. If they survived, they were sent straight to prison as soon as they had recovered. The husbands were left without a wife, and the children that they already had were left without a mother. Then the husbands would scarper, and the State would move the children into its wretched orphanages. In other words, even the children that escaped abortion were not wanted. People in Romania still talk to this day of the generation of '*decreței*' – decree babies.

The regime managed to control even the most private matters. Intimacy was nationalised. Women were forcibly examined using insidious methods: for example, they needed a certificate from the gynaecologist in order to get access to dental treatment.

One gets the impression that sexuality often served as an outlet. The men – and women – pant at love, at life. You often use the term 'cravings' in this context.

Despite all the coercion, attitudes to sexuality remained permissive. It was almost the only thing you could do with your desire. Unheated offices, power cuts, patriotic choirs on the loudspeakers, bad food, tedious meetings and political control do not make people frigid – on the contrary, they become bent on feeling something. Eroticism was a compensation for all the freedoms people were lacking. The surface was disciplined, but I had the impression that political obedience heightened people's desire. There was a high predisposition towards sex right across the professional classes; arousal grew out of people's melancholy. Both boredom and hopelessness called for distraction. You were constantly in the factory, and you didn't have any free weekends, and so there were hidden sexual relations cutting across all hierarchies. It's not that these relationships were pure eroticism though, they were a knot of seduction and calculation – or blackmail. And they led to aberrations which were later regretted, as well as deceit, humiliation and despair. Scores were settled mercilessly. These affairs might arise out of a sudden opportunity to make an advance, or through more gradual manoeuvring. Sometimes one person had fallen head over heels in love, while for the other it was all just a means to an end: a path to better pay and a higher-ranking position.

There was a lot of greed back then, too – whether other people's or one's own. It permeated all registers of feeling. This is probably nothing remarkable, it's like anywhere else in the world. And yet I believe that desire grew faster and crashed harder in Romania. It's easy to destroy relationships from within. But ours were destroyed from without, too. They were always within reach of the regime; they were exposed, politically. And for this reason, they seldom remained intact. I believe that all our external circumstances participate in our feelings; all of us carried within us the pattern of dictatorship, even in love.

*We have talked about the lunatics on the street, about
the dangers they were exposed to. Your grandmother
also lived in a state of insanity, but in her case it was a
freer, more cheerful kind of madness. You're a swallow,
too, she once said to the priest. I'll get changed, then
we can fly away together.*

My grandmother suffered from dementia for many years. She asked me whether I had a husband. And when I said no, she asked whether he had a hat. She looked at me and said we used to have a little girl, where is she now? She meant me, as a child. And I said: she grew up.

What is insanity? Reality is no longer there, and so a surreality appears in its place. An off-centre, very singular beauty. It hurts, it makes you anxious. I experienced this with my grandmother: how startlingly insanity combines its images and is expressed in metaphors, even by those who have never thought about language. This unknowing poetry is created. With so-called lunatics, logic resembles superstition.

In the novel *The Hunger Angel*, one of the main characters is Kati Sentry. There really was such a person in the labour camp, but Oskar Pastior* didn't know much about her. And I wanted her to play a central role in the novel. So she is the one for whom I invented the most things: dialogue, situations. Pastior had told me only general things; he had no personal relationship with her, I don't think anybody did. It was probably the same in the camp as it was with the dwarf lady on the monument square, or the man with the bouquet: Kati Sentry didn't even know where she was, but wherever she was, she was sufficient unto

---

*　Oskar Pastior (1927–2006) was a Romanian German poet, and the only Romanian member of Oulipo – a mainly French group of writers and mathematicians formed in the 1960s, who produce texts by imposing strict rules on themselves (a famous example being Georges Perec's novel *La Disparition*, written entirely without using the letter 'e'). His experience of deportation to a Soviet forced labour camp provided much of the material behind Herta Müller's novel *The Hunger Angel*.

herself. Oskar Pastior was very honest, he wasn't sugar-coating anything when he said: 'We all liked her, not for her sake, but for our own – because we knew that for as long as we guaranteed her survival, we had not yet entirely lost our humanity.' In other words, mad Kati Sentry was a yardstick for regular people. That inspired me a lot when I had to construct situations for this character. And I knew those situations; I would draw from memories of my grandmother. I wasn't creating a carbon copy, though. Instead, through invention I conjured up a felt reality. I was very moved by Kati Sentry, she became my favourite person as I wrote.

Do you have a husband? No. Does he have a hat? I really did have this conversation with my grandmother. The priest being a swallow, that she could fly away with him – that I invented. She also never told my grandfather that his heart-beast was a mouse; I also invented that, for the textual version of my grandmother. These inventions are moving, but they are not written for the real person – or for myself, for that matter. Of course, thinking back to my real grandmother protects me while I am writing, but nevertheless I am not inventing anything *for her* – I am doing it out of necessity for the text. And what protects you most while you are writing is also what wears you out most. The two even each other out, there is no protection left.

> *The first-person narrator gets to know the lunatics because – abandoned as she is – she has become used to wandering through the city. The only companions she has left are the people who live on the street and the friends who live in the same state of fear as she does – is there nobody else?*

Yes, the wandering. The first-person narrator isn't me. But I too would walk aimlessly through the streets, in order not to fall back into myself. I had been thrown out of the factory, I was unemployed and had no idea how I was supposed to make a living. When your feet walk themselves to the point of exhaustion, your head clears. The streetscape is different every day, every hour even, but no matter how it appears it always carries you away from yourself. It is precisely when you have lost your hold on anything that you shouldn't be alone; you should avoid locking yourself up at home. It is better to look at the summer in other people's gardens, or the snow on other people's fences. I forced myself to go out somewhere in the city every day. Often to remote neighbourhoods.

For three years, I had taken a tram to the factory every morning. It travelled down a long, dirty street, and every morning I would see a big brown dog sitting there, sometimes to the left of the front door, sometimes to its right, and sometimes aslant on the concrete steps. After my dismissal, I once walked along this route. And when I stood before the building with the brown dog, I saw it from very close up. I felt betrayed. The dog was made out of plaster. And I asked myself why the people living inside this building positioned it differently every day. Was the dog supposed to look alive and protect the house? Or did they just find it pretty, an oversized knick-knack? And who was it that was moving the plaster dog and when did they do it – in the morning after getting up or in the evening before going to sleep? Or was it moved inside at night? In short, the so-called normal people of the city were often more mysterious than the lunatics. I never saw the owner of the plaster dog. Nor did I return to the building. Even if, back then, as I stood with my nose pressed up to the fence, someone had come out of the building, I would not have spoken to them. I felt uneasy, almost nauseous. I don't know why, but I was afraid of the plaster dog. It reflected something that had to do with me. Just like the dahlias, the plaster dog revealed something that could not be said with words. But, unlike the plants, it was threatening. That dog was another of the city's background artists and, just like the lunatics, it held within it the whole picture.

Once you become an enemy of the State, the only friends you have left are people in the same situation you are in. Even when a new acquaintance enters your life, for anyone who is your friend is soon also seen as an enemy of the State. This is why most people avoid you. Your neighbours, your colleagues. If we were to look at my Securitate file now, we would see that all the neighbours who still spoke to me at that time had been assigned to inform on me. After I was thrown out of the factory, the only jobs I secured were temporary positions at various schools, and it wasn't long before I was dismissed again. Wherever I was, I didn't know any of my colleagues and so I had to assume that the Securitate would set informers on to me. It became entirely normal for me to view every approach made by another person from this perspective, to assess that person in order to protect myself – anything else would have been negligent, unforgivably foolish in fact.

It was like this for all my friends. When one of us was summoned to an interrogation, we all waited on their return. Then, while everything remained fresh in their head, they would describe the interrogation to us, right down to the smallest detail. Then we would write down minutes from memory. For the exact content of the interrogations was equally important to all of us. Sooner or later, the next person would be called in and they needed to know what answers their friends had given and stick to them as best they could. It was also important to take note of what you yourself had said: on no account should one contradict oneself.

I continued to meet up with my friend Jenny after I was dismissed from the factory. I told her about everything that had happened to our entire group, aside from the interrogations – the house searches and staged break-ins, the pretrial detention, the dismissals, etc. Although she knew my history at the factory very well, she found it difficult to imagine the whole situation. What do they want from you, she once asked me. Fear, I said.

You speak repeatedly of a 'planned fear' which you and your friends lived in. You were surveilled, your flats were searched, the secret service started to harass your parents; the pressure was progressively increased. How far is fear something that can be shared?

You can share it, but this does not lessen its force. Really, you are just helping it spread among you. And fear does this of its own accord anyway when you are friends with someone. You know all about each other, you are constantly together. And this somewhat protects you: on your own, the fear feels insurmountable, it can devour you. But even with the protection of friendship, fear remains unavoidable: it comes from outside, from persecution, and cannot be prevented, however close you are to your friends; your fear is confirmed every day through new and repeated acts of harassment. There are different kinds of fear: a brief one, which flares up and disappears again right away, and a chronic, protracted fear, which stays with you. There is plain fear, churning and ruthless, but there is also level-headed fear, when you're at once overwrought and jaded, alternating between hyperbole and trivialising the source of your fear. All the adjectives don't describe it, of course – however, one can but list words, how else are we supposed to talk about feelings? Fears flash through a spectrum and colour everything, they infiltrate all your other emotions. When you are afraid, you do not look for words to describe your fear. And even if you were to find them, they wouldn't change anything. But sometimes you do know with hindsight what kind of fear you were feeling. Or one of your friends will tell you.

It helps if someone you trust looks at your fear. Someone who can recognise what state you are in. This has nothing to do with talking about the fear, though; I think people should talk as little as possible about fear. You should not constantly address it by name, because this only feeds it. It must disappear every so often, so that you can live with it. If this no longer happens, then you lose your mind. This is why friends are so important, because, through their closeness, one friend enables the other to suppress their fear.

When you were together, what did you do? Were you able to outwit the fear, at least for a short while?

When we were together, we came up with all sorts of strategies. We told each other jokes, we played around with rhyming sentences for hours, we sang Ceaușescu's speeches out of the newspaper in the style of operettas. Rhyming and singing infiltrate the skull. As a child, I would continue to hear the sound of the brass band long after leaving a village wedding, even when I was home, lying in my bed. In the same way, I continued to hear our operetta songs and rhyming games in my head for hours afterwards. And this would continue over the following days; I would rhyme as I strayed through the city, alone. A rhyme doesn't let up, it builds an echo in your temples. It constantly calls for new rhymes in your head, and you find yourself hauling around new pairs of words with you wherever you go, testing their weak, senseless rhymes. I was fed up with it all, I was tired and yet I didn't stop. There was something that was at once excruciating and protective about this rhyming disease.

Often we would play the christened fly game. We would give a fly the name of a secret service agent. We would then switch off the light in the room it was in, and switch on the light in the room we were in, and beckon it in, calling it by its name. We would do this over and over again, and the fly would come flying across to us every time. There was no magic involved, just the mundane, dependable law that flies will always come out of the darkness and into the light. But it looked like black magic. We had scared fear away, we had laughed ourselves free. What joy. A fear-driven joy, perhaps, but one which lasted for hours on end. And one that was contributing to our own destruction – but we didn't know that at the time. We didn't know we were being listened in on day and night and that all the rooms in our flat were bugged. We had learnt the fastest routes to happiness, how to jump from naught to sixty through foolishness. We all knew the causes of our misery. And not one of them was under our control. So our joy needed no cause, only this sense that we urgently depended on it. Our joy hinged on its spontaneity, and it was a necessary mischief.

Yes, as long as you occasionally get some respite from the fear, you will not fall to pieces: you know this from your own experience, and you see it in other people, too. Everyone wanted to prevent themselves and others from breaking down. But friendships are no guarantee of this. We all saw friends fall apart, situations where even the most intimate friendship couldn't save the individuals involved. A friend's fear could be shared out between us all, but if it started to whir on a different wavelength in their head, then they were beyond saving. And the threats would keep coming.

I knew the shimmer of this other wavelength well. Perhaps I knew it from when I was a child, from the melon heart of the Blessed Mary, and later from the corpse sugar of the lime trees and from the fridge in my halls of residence with its heart-beast, and from the handkerchief office in the factory. And yet fear never swallowed me up entirely. I was confused, yet I also remained clear-headed. That other wavelength only ever managed to creep into half of my mind, thank God.

You and your friends were dependent on each other, precisely because you all found yourselves facing the same danger. 'But in our quarrels,' you write, '[love] grew claws.' This great intimacy, from which one could no longer disengage, was presumably not always easy to bear.

Our friendships were tight, and relationships aren't always easy when one person is dependent on the other. Our tone with one another often became harsh; we had thin nerves. Sometimes, things were so fraught that even kindness became unbearable. We often felt rage and anger, a pain that we could not avoid inflicting on each other, due to this intimacy that we could not escape from. Criticism was meted out very directly in our group, we expected it of each other. What I found most difficult was the binge drinking.

We were sitting in a room at Rolf Bossert's,* on the fourth floor of his block of flats. It was past midnight, I heard something clatter on the balcony and ran over. Bossert had already put one leg over the side of the balcony, and his body was hanging crookedly over the edge. I wrenched him back on to the balcony and then into a chair in the kitchen. I screamed at him, what are you doing? Nothing, he said, tersely. I'm killing myself. Everyone was plastered, and in the chaos of laughter and shouting no one had noticed his absence. The following morning, I found myself alone with him in the kitchen, and he said I shouldn't have interfered. If you're going to do it, I said, then please do it when you're alone. How are your friends supposed to continue living after something like that? He wouldn't have survived the fall from the fourth floor.

Boozing turned the slightest disagreements into conflicts that could easily spiral. Our intimacy took on a dark edge; our statements began to sting, our gestures became gruff, we grew cantankerous and coarse.

Alcohol and despair are a bad mix, but a mix that is typical for all of Eastern Europe. You had to stand in a queue for half a day just to get bread or milk, you had to

____

*   Rolf Bossert (1952–86) was a Romanian writer and journalist of Banat Swabian origin and a founding member of the *Aktionsgruppe Banat*.

show your identity papers to get butter or flour, and you couldn't get hold of any meat at all. But the shop always had booze – watered-down stuff. The State-sponsored poison was the regime's anaesthetic: the more people careened around drunk, the less they would think of rebelling. And alcohol reduced people's life expectancy. It destroyed your guts so swiftly that the State was spared from having to pay out pensions to the drinkers.

When you don't drink yourself, the desperation of other people's drinking is hard to bear. I never had a drop, even long before I got to know my friends, because my father was an alcoholic and was drunk almost every day, and his boozy village songs clung to my childhood. And then when I got to know my friends, and started to feel that I belonged with them, I was still just as repelled by alcohol as I had been back then. I could see how it drowned people's understanding.

On these dark, drunken days I would distance myself from my friends in my mind. They're not stupid, it's the alcohol, I would say to myself. On many such days I was in a liminal space, I was neither one of the drunks but nor was I entirely myself. Our friendship withstood it all though; you had to siphon the drinking off where it belonged, and it belonged to despair. And by the next day the boozing would be over, and everyone would have slept off their inebriation and they'd be themselves once more. And I'd be with them again, without any distance between us. Not one of them ever reproached any of the others about their behaviour, not once. And nor did I. I really had nothing to reproach them for. I knew that if I were to drink, I would have been in the same desperate state. Where else was there to go?

Desperate and, at the same time, crazy for life . . .
In the end, fear wouldn't let go of Rolf Bossert
– his nerves snapped.

Rolf Bossert was a hunted man. Once, when he came back from town, he was out of breath and saucer-eyed. He told us how fifty secret service agents had been following him, and it was then that we knew: he'd already tuned into the other wavelength; he was paranoid. And no one could talk him out of it any more. It was painful. We wished we could lift him out of this state, but how? The Securitate's strategy continued to unfold according to plan.

It started with an assault. He was beaten up in the street, they broke his jawbone. No sooner had he been released from hospital than the house searches began, and his manuscripts and letters were confiscated. Then they got into the car with him, they wanted to drive to the passport office, his passport was ready to be picked up they said. But the car didn't go to the passport office, the driver kept stopping again and again as they drove through the city and every time another person would climb in. Bossert sat tightly squeezed between these 'friends'. Then they drove out of the city to a patch of woodland. Bossert thought they were going to shoot him. They didn't, but they showed him how easy it would be if they had wanted to. The last threshold of normality had been crossed. To every horror was added another, it was no longer to be endured. His mind snapped, and our kindness and friendship were of no use any more. Calling a doctor was out of the question: the secret service went in and out of every psychiatric ward, manipulated diagnoses and 'treated' the patients as it saw fit. If you were being politically persecuted, it was unthinkable to put yourself in the hands of a psychologist.

It makes your blood run cold – you can now glean from Bossert's file that the secret service expected him to take his own life. He was at acute risk, it says so in the file. And so he was to be allowed to leave the country early enough for his suicide to take place in the West, not in Romania. And this is exactly what then happened, three weeks after his departure, in his temporary accommodation in Frankfurt.

The case of Rolf Bossert was a terrible lesson for us all that there is a point of no return, that you should pack your suitcase while you're still in possession of your senses and can tell the difference between reality and insanity, while you are still present.

Sometimes entirely different incidents jump together through a single word they all have in common. Three incidents that marked my life come into contact with each other through the word 'finger'. In all three, the word 'finger' attracts death like a magnet.

The first incident took place just after I had arrived in the city. I was living in a sublet together with a slightly older girl from the village. She wanted to become a nurse, and so she went to nursing college after secondary school. Her work placements sometimes took place in mortuaries. One day I put my hand into my handbag in the middle of the city and pulled out a severed finger – it was indigo-blue, a souvenir from the morgue. It was someone's dead finger. The shock and revulsion. I would never forget this first finger.

The second finger. Rolf Bossert told our circle of friends, shortly before he left the country: I won't lift a finger for you once I'm gone. It was a sad and aggressive sentence, struck through with despair, with pain at his forced separation from us and his fear of arriving in Germany. To me the sentence sounded spiteful: he wouldn't lift a finger, even if the Devil came for us. Bossert never remained true to this sentence. He immediately spoke out about the crimes of the dictatorship once he was in the West – for three weeks. And then he threw himself out of a window. Even in the West, no autopsy was performed, no one requested one. It will have been suicide – he was broken enough to do it on his own – but it was authored by the Securitate, and their plan can be read in his file. Did someone perhaps 'help' him after all, that night, at the window of the shared kitchen in his temporary accommodation?

A few years later, the third finger came into play: a sentence written on Roland Kirsch's last postcard before he was found hanged in his flat: 'Sometimes I have to bite myself on the finger to feel that I still exist.' His death too was called a 'suicide', but no one believed the official death certificate.

I don't want to let the word 'finger' resurface repeatedly over the years and point at death. But three times is too many for it not to be conspicuous. Against my will, a sequence has developed with the word 'finger'. Three fingers is enough to start a tally. And one must keep count of what one knows. You can't do more than keep count, after all.

When one's nerves are not overburdened, overstretched, overstrung for a long time, do they then recover somewhat?

One's chronic fear and inner restlessness diminish. At times they disappear completely. But you remain easily disturbed, much more easily than people who have more intact nerves. After all, I don't say to myself: I'm going to have a think about the past now. The present is laced with the past, so that the past is part of our present time. I am in the present, but the past is also with me, whether I want it or not. I have to acknowledge both my present and past selves, that is all. Nothing disappears, I can't will it away or write it away. Literature does not heal anything; all I can do is look into things, over and over again, in different ways. Everyone does this in their own way with life, even when they don't write. People talk about life having been 'stolen' from them, only it seems to me that experiencing difficulty means that there is more life in your head, not less. And mostly it arrives unannounced.

All Full of Cold Feelings

In The Appointment, *you describe your journey to an interrogation. It starts with the sentence 'I've been summoned,' and explores what happens when those in power attack a person directly, what effects this has on one's head and heart and perception. First of all: how was one summoned?*

It varied. Sometimes you weren't summoned at all, and you were just picked up from wherever you happened to be.

Because dictatorships use surprise, blindsiding, unpredictability?

The fact that the secret service of a surveillance state is constantly acting against you is no surprise. Once you have their attention and are suspected of being an enemy of the State, then that is what you remain. But their course of action would still be a surprise. The objective of the secret service was the 'disintegration' of the person, and it was the same for all 'enemies'. But they looked for different methods to achieve this for each individual and found those which would harm this person most. The dosage and destructive potential of the attacks were calculated precisely. The Securitate was a colossal Fear Station, with psychologically trained fear experts and their fearsome methods, and with a variety of short and long-term plans, just like the Socialist economy. But unlike in the economy, these plans were actually implemented. The only productive sector of the economy under Socialism was the production of fear. And the secret service was, if you look at it cynically, the only institution in the country that attended to the individual – only, it did this in order to destroy them.

The secret service's general intention to break you was clear, but the intention of each individual attack was opaque. You wanted to understand, and so you had to analyse every detail of the interrogation and try and map it against the wider picture. The wider picture both for yourself and for your group of friends. For we belonged together as a result of our friendship, but also because we were grouped together in the plans of the Securitate. When one of the group was being 'disintegrated', each of us felt the effects of it and could trace how it was planned and implemented. The faster it was triggered, the faster it shook everyone else to the core.

One's confrontation with the secret service was sometimes direct, sometimes covert and sometimes hidden. The interrogations were direct.

Invading your flat and leaving behind signs was a covert form of confrontation – a picture that hung on your wall would be left lying on your bed, a shoe would be on top of the fridge, or a kitchen stool would be in your bedroom, but the door to your flat would be intact. You were supposed to understand that they had a key, that they could come in at any moment if they wanted to, including when you were at home. You were as readily available to them in your bedroom as you were outside on the street. Staying home did not give you any security whatsoever. Your flat was no longer private.

The most uncanny sign the secret service left
behind was the cut-up fox.

In my bedroom, between my bed and my wardrobe, lay my fox fur. I had bought it with my mother, from a hunter in the neighbouring village. The village tailor was supposed to turn it into a collar and cuffs for a coat. He was a very flat fox with a muzzle and paws and shiny claws – he was far too beautiful to be cut into pieces. I kept him for many years as a rug. One day, I was mopping the floor in my room and the fox's tail slipped to one side. It had been cut off. At the time, I managed to convince myself that it had become detached by accident. But I didn't believe myself really: it hadn't been torn at all, the 'tear' was perfectly straight, it had been neatly cut; it was scrupulous work. I laid the tail back on the pelt. Then, a few weeks later, one of the hind legs was cut off, then later the second, then the front feet, one after another. They were always left placed on top of the fox's belly. This went on for months. I became used to checking whether anything had been cut off the fox as soon as I came home. I too would leave the amputated parts lying where they were. Living with this dismembered fox, my whole flat felt like a trap. But I didn't want to throw him away, I thought that as long as they were fixated on the fox they would spare me.

A hidden confrontation was invading your flat without leaving behind any signs. My flat was also bugged back then, for example. The microphones had been installed underneath our floorboards, accessed through the ceiling of the flat beneath ours. There was a name plate on the door to that flat, but no one lived there. It seems to have been used purely as a surveillance station by the secret service.

This all seems ridiculous, but it's recorded in the files. None of us would have thought that the Securitate would have gone to such lengths on our account – that this regime would cling to its animosities with such paranoia and would wear itself out so absurdly on a daily basis.

But by summoning you to an interrogation, the secret service was blowing its cover. How did this happen? Did you receive a letter, did a man ring at your door? Was the next interrogation always announced at the end of the previous one?

We were summoned to interrogations orally, never in writing, so that we would have no evidence. We lived in a block of flats, on the fifth floor. There would be a knock at the door, and a man in a greasy suit would be standing there – a messenger. He would say: tomorrow, or in three days' time, or next week, at such and such a time, at the secret service offices. All of it orally, he had no papers on him, he needed no signature, he did not wait for an answer. Day, time, secret service offices – the messenger would say this handful of words and then he'd be gone. And I would close the door and my head would start to churn, wondering what it would be about this time. You wanted to be prepared. You would discuss countless scenarios with your friends. You would read through the previous minutes again, turning over potential questions and thinking up answers to them. We thought at the time that we were keeping each other informed, that this was helpful. The secret service was probably amused by our 'preparations' and our naivety: we know now that the flat had been bugged, that every conversation was listened in on. We thought we were protecting one another, helping each other by swapping tricks and bits of advice. Instead, we were unwittingly delivering ourselves up to the microphone. It's awful: we had revealed everything to the secret service by the time we arrived for our interrogation. Every time you were summoned, you would contemplate what would happen if you simply didn't turn up. But they would have come for you, wherever you were hiding. There was nowhere to hide. And making them come for you would have meant you'd be locked up.

The worst interrogations were when you hadn't been summoned at all but were fished off the street. I was going to the hairdresser's once. On my way through the park, a policeman 'happened' to come up to me, asking for my identity papers. He glanced at them and said: come with me. He had an Alsatian with him, a baton and a gun. He brought me to the basement of a student hall of residence. It was a long, narrow room in which three other guys were waiting for me. The policeman gave my identity papers to a tanned, gaunt man with a golden incisor in his mouth – he was their boss. He kept dropping my papers on the ground and I had to pick them up and give them back to him. He did this dozens of times, and if I didn't bend down quickly enough he would kick me in the small of the back or on my backside. He said I was a prostitute, a bitch on heat, that I had had sexual relations with eight Arab students and had been paid in cosmetic products and pairs of tights. So we meet again, baby doll, he said. I had never seen him before. The Securitate is constantly following me around, I said, they know that I don't know a single Arab. You know twenty of them, if we want you to, he said. You'll see, it'll be an interesting trial. He had a raspy laugh. And when he started laughing, the other two would follow suit, much like how, if one dog barks, the others join in. They would laugh louder than him and for longer, so that he was flattered and the sound would linger. I had to eat eight hard-boiled eggs with onions and coarse salt from the long table they were sitting at. A woman's voice was screaming through a closed door at the back of the room. I made an effort not to show my fear and choked the food down, hoping that the voice was just being played from a tape.

As far as my friends were concerned, I was at the hairdresser's. Nobody knew that I had ended up in the hands of the secret service. I could have disappeared and never resurfaced again. Nobody would have guessed what had happened and where I had ended up. There were many such mysteries in the country, as many as there were clandestine locations used by the secret service – a labyrinth of torture scattered across cities and the countryside. Hundreds of hotel rooms, extorted flats, sheds – rooms of all kinds. Once I was at the market buying nuts and I was hauled away from there to a backyard in which there were several woodsheds. I had allegedly paid too much for the nuts, undermining the State's standard pricing. But there was no standard price – the State didn't have any nuts. In one of these woodsheds, a guy sat behind a typewriter and was writing up a report about what I was guilty of. The ten customers before me had bought the nuts at the same price, and the nuts cost exactly the same after me. And the farmer who was selling them was a private salesman. It was pure harassment, based on entirely fabricated reasons. I refused to sign the freshly typed report. A few weeks later, I received a court summons. But then they kicked the whole thing into the long grass.

Being fished from the street was my greatest fear. My second greatest was a sham trial – a real conviction with phoney evidence and blackmailed witnesses.

But why these theatrics? Why did they not simply say: you have written books that we consider to be dangerous, you express political opinions that we can no longer tolerate?

My interrogator never said: you are an enemy of the people. And he never said: you criticise Socialism in your texts. He cited prostitution and bootlegging as the grounds for my harassment, conjuring them out of thin air. He had also, apparently, 'discovered' content that was 'decadent' and 'pornographic' in my books. After being thrown out of the factory, I was viewed as 'parasitic', because unemployment did not exist. There was a right to work and a duty to work. And as the Socialist proverb goes: anyone who does not work should not eat either.

A parasite, a prostitute, a bootlegger – as far as I was concerned, it was all absurd theatrics, because it had nothing to do with reality. But for the Securitate these were devious chess moves, they were not absurd at all. Prostitution and bootlegging were prohibited; either would land you in prison. This was why they had dreamt up these particular offences. The intention was to make me understand that, by law, they could arrest me any day, but that they were not doing so just yet. I was supposed to live in a state of uncertainty, while still walking around freely for the time being. They wanted it to hang over me constantly, to make me buckle.

This was a tactic that was thought through, right down to the last detail: my political position was not addressed in any of the interrogations, and the fact that I had refused to become an informer for the Securitate was never mentioned either. Instead, these invented offences were pored over for hours, as though they were a reality: the places where I had supposedly sold my illegal wares, the names of sellers. The secret service was constructing an alibi for itself by shifting my 'offence' from that of a dissident into general criminality: instead of owning up to its own political repression, the secret service defined *me* as a criminal. Thus, instead of being an apparatus for repression, the State was simply combating prostitution and pornography – and was therefore concerned about propriety and moral values in the country. It denied its political persecution in order to avoid any substantive discussion about the dictatorship. If there had been any discussion about the dictatorship, we would have had to talk about the regime during the interrogation and we would have gone into details, into reality. The authorities were not going to do that to themselves, they had no need to. Their cowardice was perfidious: denying the political motives behind this repression laid bare both the self-denial and self-importance of the secret service. For I had to go along with the show, talking for whole half-days about the rubbish they had invented: where I had supposedly engaged in bootlegging, sellers whose names I had never heard before.

You were taken away from yourself and forced into

being this fabricated person instead. You were set in front of this huge, boundless lie and you sat there, cut off from your own mind. The interrogator was advantaged by this lie, he would gesticulate, knock on his big, polished table. I thought: there's a madhouse beneath his scalp. He was not the slightest bit embarrassed, even though he knew that I knew that everything I had to explain away was a fabrication. And he knew that I knew why he did not want to talk about the regime. He was proud to belong to the dictatorship so seamlessly. It's not that he was a representative of it while he interrogated me, but rather that he *was* the dictatorship. It was no mere room that the door to his office opened into and closed off, but the dictatorship itself. He had an oily scalp, his fingernails were like pumpkin seeds and, when he stretched his feet diagonally under his desk, I saw his plaster-white calves. I could see how no hair was growing on those calves, how already age was smoothing them, and I often thought: he's living on borrowed time, no dictatorship can help him – he too will die. And I was so sure that I enjoyed living, and that my life would not be shortened because of him. But at the same time, I saw the many marks – codes, circles, numbers, lines – engraved into the small interrogation table I was sitting at. These were the traces of fear, from those who had been interrogated before me. And I felt such grief, as if they had all left their hopelessness in my chair. As though, when I was sitting there, I was less myself and more a composite of all of us who had been interrogated.

He gave no answer when I asked why he was keeping quiet about the real motives for my persecution. He did the same when I asked why he never pronounced the dictator's name, but used instead a ponderous *'he'* when he meant

Ceauşescu. He grinned when I asked: how long would the secret service serve a regime that let its people starve? And when I asked whether he knew that oddments from the stocking factory were used as bandages on surgical wards, and whether he cared at all about the Romanian people. Eventually, he said I thought you were an intelligent girl, condescendingly. Only then did he start to scream about how I was against the Romanian people, yet still had the gall to eat Romanian bread. Why don't you just emigrate, you can join the other German fascists and become a whore in the capitalist swamp?

All government agencies, particularly the secret service, had a problem with the Constitution. The Romanian Constitution was the most subversive text ever. The more the regime infringed our human rights, the more it hid away its Constitution. You couldn't read the text of the Constitution anywhere, you couldn't get hold of it in any library, in any bookshop, in any antiquarian bookshop. Anyone who somehow still had it from earlier in the Socialist era was in possession of a secret document. According to the Constitution, there was freedom of opinion, freedom of the press, privacy of correspondence, freedom of assembly. Freedom of travel, even – everyone is allowed to leave any country, it said, including their own. And yet, those who tried to flee Romania were torn to shreds by specially trained dogs at the border or were shot dead or were pulverised by the propellers of ships in the Danube. In the cereal fields along the border, the farmers would end up with half-putrefied corpses in their combine harvesters. Nobody knows the number of people who died trying to escape. There were thousands, but, to this day, this topic is still not talked about in Romania. I know from doctors that every day, seriously injured people were brought into hospital from the border, but that upon arrival they were 'treated' by the secret service first. If they bled to death during their interrogation, the doctor would write 'heart attack', 'stroke' or whatever on the death certificate. But just as often there wasn't even a death to record: countless people neither arrived back home nor in another country, they simply disappeared from the face of the Earth without leaving a trace. The Securitate didn't only have a secret empire of fear for the living, it also had a labyrinth of graveyards in which to hastily bury people. Despite this, escape remained an obsession among the people because life was so miserable. We all knew gruesome stories about people who had died trying to escape. An attempt to escape is two-thirds suicide: that was what people said, but then you did it anyway. People were broken; death didn't scare them off. They were facing either a ruined life or no life at all; those that chose to escape didn't care. Apart from poverty, this desire to escape was the second major feature everyone had in common in the country. People were literally dying to escape. 'Freedom of travel'! The regime violated the Constitution every day.

One wonders why it wasn't amended, tailored to fit the repression. I believe this too was about self-importance; it simply wasn't necessary. In order to amend the Constitution, they would have to acknowledge the repression, as well as put it into words. And then the dictatorship would have been reflected in the text of the Constitution. But in this old Constitution stuffed full of liberties, democracy ruled. The regime needed the Constitution in order to fend off criticism from the West. As for any domestic criticism — they couldn't have cared less.

The interrogations drew on a whole dramaturgy: there were elements that were repeated, like greeting you with a kiss on the hand, and others that varied, like the name-calling and ways of putting pressure on you. How much latitude did the interrogator have?

There wasn't always a kiss on the hand when you arrived, but often there was. With a deliberately half-open mouth and with spittle. My heart would freeze each time, until he let go of my hand. I mustn't twitch, or allow myself to wipe away the saliva. After this perversion of a decorous gesture, he would switch register, calling me a whore and a bitch on heat. He needed this mix of sham courtesy and contempt to heighten my humiliation. He knew that I would have preferred an honest slap in the face to a phoney kiss on the hand.

The substance of their allegations, however, was always repeated – vile assertions, vulgar invectives and invented accusations. The dates, the persons involved, all of it was entirely fabricated, but precisely described and alarmingly plausible – they had decided that the street that led to the prison was the location for my bootlegging. I had to dispute these fabrications for hours and yet it was never any use. They stuck doggedly to their allegations, and threw in some racism for good measure – prostitution with Romanians wasn't enough for the Securitate, it had to be Arab men I was selling myself to.

I was the only woman in our circle of friends. The accusation of prostitution also helped them discredit the group. What will you do if you have a red-haired child? the interrogator asked. Three of our friends had reddish hair. I said: you don't get pregnant from talking. 'Group sex' was an accusation that was only ever directed at me, it was never brought up with my friends. This was the mentality of the Securitate: something that men are allowed to do is a source of ignominy for women. And this group sex narrative had to specifically culminate in me falling pregnant with the child of one of my red-haired friends. It made the whole thing juicier for them – my interrogator's lips grew narrow and angular with revulsion at the thought. He was entitled to elaborately display his disgust, of course. My revulsion for him was just as great, but I couldn't let him notice this.

I always had the same interrogator. And when there were several, he was always one of them. The premises sometimes changed, though. Aside from his office with the big polished desk, he might take me to a smaller room with no windows and a small desk. This one only had a chair for me, and no interrogation table. You couldn't prop your arms on anything, you had to sit up straight, with your whole body exposed. And so your fear visibly hung from you, from your forehead to your toes. Who knows what the point of changing the room was. Once I was taken to a room full of rows of seats, like a cinema auditorium. Sometimes the interrogator would bring me to a room and leave. It was as if he had forgotten about me, I was waiting for so long. It was like back in the days when the accordion teacher would abandon me to go out to his garden.

Sometimes my interrogator would walk out in the middle of the interrogation, leaving me alone. I would sit and stare into space. I tried to do nothing. Not to pace up and down, not to sigh, not to touch my face with my hands too often. It was excruciating to do nothing. How do you do nothing? Doubtless there were hidden cameras observing my growing nervousness.

During an interrogation, you had to agree to the terms of the conversation, no matter how ludicrously impertinent and dishonest the whole thing was.

'You learn as you go,' you write, 'but I can't show that I'm learning.'

You couldn't answer too curtly, that drove the interrogator to fits of rage. You had to let him feel his own power, otherwise he became uncomfortable to be around. If your answers were too short, he had more time to ask you questions. But it was just as risky to give him long answers. You couldn't say too much, no more than was absolutely necessary. You had to avoid accidentally suggesting questions to him that he would not have asked otherwise. And as you incessantly regurgitated the same statements, you had to be careful not to introduce any other version of events. No straying off course, always repeat what you yourself or your friends have already said. To protect ourselves, we did also lie. We had our common lies and each person's individual lies. And they all had to be maintained.

You couldn't be intractable, but nor could you be subservient. I don't know whether the word 'amenable' describes it. Every interrogation remained inscrutable to us – its sense, its purpose. For the most part I didn't even know whether I had stood my ground or failed to notice the traps that had been set for me. The interrogation resembled an exchange of blows, but in reality it was no such thing. Because for us, there was nothing at all to be gained. I never thought that I had come out of an interrogation appearing more innocent than when I went in. Nor did I think that one day they would suspect me less. You knew that you would always remain an enemy of the State; the regime had to arbitrarily invent enemies in order to present its repression as a necessity. The only way I could have changed my status would have been to work as an informer.

In the summer, it was still light on my way home from the interrogation. I would always walk, because of the plants. I felt my brain inside my skull when I saw the blossom. And in the trees the leaves were ruffled and weary and showed me where I had just come from. And in the dark winter the sky was perforated by an abundance of stars. Whoever dresses cleanly cannot arrive in Heaven dirty: I often had the interrogator's sentence in my head while the stars glittered in the black heavens. I saw the brightly lit trams as rooms driving around. People sat at the windows as if they were on display. I felt transparent, I would never have got on one of them. On the way there and back I would recite poems and song lyrics to the beat of my steps: 'World, world, sister world, when will I have had enough of you . . .' I was a shaky imitation of myself, losing myself in these surreal associations did me good. I walked as if guided by an invisible hand: from the normality of the street into the insanity of the interrogation; then, in the evening, out of the insanity and on to the street.

You describe two ways of getting ready for the interrogation. In one, the protagonist tries to find something to hold on to through a precise ritual. She climbs out of bed with her right foot first, she always wears the same blouse and she eats a walnut before leaving her flat. Her boyfriend Paul thinks it is more important to prepare for the questions, to which she responds that they always ask different ones.

You still prepared, though. You would be milling through it all in your head for every minute of the days leading up to the interrogation. You had to, it was part of the process. From the moment the messenger told you at the door that you were summoned, your head was already inside the interrogation.

There were more harmless interrogation sessions, during which you were there 'so the clock didn't tick on into the void.' You were spared from open threats, violations and violence.

There were no harmless episodes, they only *seemed* harmless – monotonous, dull. But this wasn't reassuring, it was oppressive. Even when the interrogation stalled, slowed down or was interrupted, this was planned. Well, perhaps the more turbulent moments weren't planned – the slaps in the face, or having your hair pulled, the screams and curses. Accidents happened; my interrogator wasn't a machine after all. And nor was I. We disdained each other, it was all about our feelings. He had his hatred, just as I did, but where I had fear, he had power. He had the script, while I never knew where an interrogation was going to go next.

There was a law according to which you could only be held until eight o'clock in the evening if you had not actually been arrested. We would invoke this when the clock struck eight: it's eight o'clock – if you don't have an arrest warrant I should be allowed to go home now.

Were these moments when you forgot your fear?
Weren't you provoking them with such a sentence?

A sentence like that worked – it's an example of the incomprehensible balance one had to strike between dignity and docility.

*Is it precisely in undignified situations that one
must insist on dignity?*

Being subservient was bad – it would only have exposed me even more to his tyrannical whims. It was better to insist on certain things, like the eight o'clock law, or to mention the Constitution. In doing so you showed that you respected yourself. You would probably have been allowed to go home anyway because his shift finished at eight and he too wanted to clock off. Nevertheless, it made a different impression if you invoked the law to secure your release, rather than appealing to his authority. Of course, he could have flouted this law, as he could any other, but that was not the point. The point was self-assertion, even if it was only for the sake of appearances. Even fear retains its dignity.

There is a scene in The Appointment *that turns
everything on its head: strategy, proportionality,
the distribution of power. The interrogator loses his
temper, the first-person narrator expects to be hit, but
instead he picks a strand of hair off her shoulder and
he goes to let it fall. And she says: 'Put the hair back,
it belongs to me.'*

You can't think up a sentence like that in advance, it comes suddenly, when you are absolutely broken inside. I was so confused – he shot towards me, screaming, and

I was braced for a slap or for him to pull my hair. Then he stood in front of my little table, twisted his face into a smile, and picked a hair off my shoulder with his fingertips. I said, quicker than I could think: please put the hair back, it belongs to me. And he really did put the hair back on my shoulder before walking across the office to the window. He looked out and laughed hysterically at his own humiliation.

You talk about a 'dumb sense of satisfaction' . . .

He could have taken revenge for this sentence. But he had lost his stride. The sentence was braver than I was, it had slipped out of me. I didn't feel satisfaction until he was standing at the window, as I saw that he had no desire to punish me for the incident. I had said please, after all: please put the hair back. My little display of courage was awful: it was a plea.

*If you had to characterise the man or men who
tormented you in this way, how would you
describe them?*

In terms of their behaviour and their mentality, all the representatives of the regime that I met were the same. Unconditionally servile when looking up, brutal when looking down. And they were narrow-minded, heavy-handed, unscrupulous, cynical, capricious, horrifyingly uneducated. They didn't need to be knowledgeable about anything of course, not even about Communism. But they knew how to take advantage of a situation. They were recruited in the 1950s as young guys from the poorest regions, half-illiterates, and Stalinistically instructed by the Soviets. Their backwardness, prudery, nationalism and peasant doltishness, with an inclination towards brutality, were simply coated in Party ideology. They had not yet acquired any material wealth but they were political parvenus, and a propensity towards violence was the best capital for their advancement. All the authorities were structured according to the Soviet model, and cadres were trained in Moscow. This first generation of functionaries existed until the last – until 1989. Even when the direct influence of Moscow abated in the 1970s, the structures didn't change: the next generation of functionaries were trained up as new cadres with the old characteristics. They too had nothing urbane, nothing cosmopolitan about them. They remained peasants, even with their polished desks, suits and ties. In the winter they wore karakul hats made with crinkly wool. And for the hot summers, when it was over thirty degrees in the shade, the functionaries had their mustard-green suits with big breast pockets and short-sleeved jackets, which they'd been wearing for decades. They were embarrassing; a stiff Socialist idea of 'summer elegance'. On top of this sense of 'big city fashion', the comrades also acquired a certain shiftiness: the oblique look, the broad gestures, the unctuous smile, the impertinent speech and vulgar swagger of shysters. Even after the collapse of the regime, right up to this day in fact, the Socialist representative of authoritarianism has remained true to himself, both in behaviour and mentality. Take a look at Putin: it's all there.

The secret service agent who was 'responsible' for me came from this first generation of cadres. He was definitely over fifty years old, and so must have worked for the secret service during the dark years of Stalin's rule. When he started his career the camps and prisons were full, and the interrogations were merciless: people were tortured, murdered. I often wondered how many tonnes of fear he had already produced for the regime, and how many people had already passed through his hands. And how merciful he believed himself to be when, between the porter's lodge and his office, he decided to give me a warning. The secret service building was a long, narrow concrete block. At one end was the entrance to the secret service, at the other was the passport office. And inside they were connected to one another. A long corridor with windows led to his office, and in the courtyard they had their own petrol pump. One day, in the corridor, he told me I shouldn't go on like this any more, otherwise they would have to kill me. He couldn't do anything about it, the instructions had come from Bucharest. Are you trying to protect me? I said. But you've summoned me in order to torture me. That's your job, isn't it? I felt uncomfortable about having to give him such short shrift. I almost felt sorry for him. Perhaps he really was warning me . . . Or was this also just a trap? Aside from disdain, vengeance and hate, did he have other feelings that he was not allowed to display? At any rate, he was taking a risk by speaking to me like that.

*Could it be conceivable that this man had developed
a relationship to you that was not just guided by a lust
for power and violence? Or was the warning part of
his repertoire a trick aimed at obtaining a certain
level of cooperation?*

I don't think so. He wasn't expecting my reaction to be any different to what he was used to from me. Perhaps his job did sometimes strike him as sordid. Everyone has feelings, after all, and they are fickle – they can jump. There was emotion involved in every phase of the interrogation. You can't separate thinking and feeling. The Securitate's elaborately devised plans for disintegration had to be implemented – meaning they had to be applied to and by actual human beings. Disdain, humiliation, vengeance, violence – there was a procedure based on every one of these words. And this procedure would reflect what the mood was in the room at that particular moment. The content of the interrogation was predefined, but not the nuances of feeling that it would inspire. I think these determined whether things remained at the level of screaming or whether they escalated to a slap in the face. Emotion played a big role.

The interrogator and I were full of disdain for each other. A single moment of compassion wasn't going to disrupt his plan for my disintegration. This warning, if indeed that is what it was, moved me. But there wasn't even a hint of a possibility of complicity with my interrogator.

This conversation happened very late, in 1984 or 1985. *Nadirs* had already come out in Germany and I had, entirely unexpectedly, won some literary prizes. Doubtless that also played a role.

*Would you have wanted to have a confrontation
with him after the fall of the regime?*

No. What was I supposed to do with a man from the secret service – and what does confrontation mean? I had had more than enough of that. We would have needed an institution to mediate any encounter – either a Public

Prosecution Service investigating the crimes of the dictatorship, or a Truth Commission like in South Africa.

But my interrogator – so I have heard from Romanian friends – returned to the region of his birth in the guise of an innocent old-age pensioner. He was never prosecuted. He came from the impoverished south, from Oltenia. His service in Banat was far enough away from where he grew up; he flew under the radar. The police, military and secret service were always sent to remote districts, so that the repression they meted out wouldn't be softened by their social ties. It guaranteed that they would carry out their dirty work for the State daily without any scruples.

But once the institution has gone, once power has gone . . . Did you feel no need at all to reverse the power dynamic, at least for the length of a conversation?

What would I have had to discuss with my interrogator in retrospect? Should I have asked him who hanged Roland Kirsch and why? Would he want to answer? Would he even be allowed to? The Securitate was a criminal organisation. To this day, no agent, whether young or old, has had to answer for the secret service's crimes. And the power of the institution has not disappeared: many young Securitate agents were transferred to the new secret service. The older ones who were discarded now receive higher than average pensions. My nerves are too dear to me for me to willingly meet former or current secret service agents. Should I now sit and listen to them telling me that they didn't ruin me, but rather protected me, since I, unlike others, am not dead? I have dead friends and know enough ruined people, lives broken by defamation, persecution and prison. I can read my file now, but the names of the secret service staff involved have been expunged from it. My file doesn't mention my three years in the factory either.

I have a huge pile of wiretap transcripts, they include all sorts of people who were inside my flat, even if it was the only time they visited me. But there isn't a single page about Roland Kirsch, who visited me every day. Why not? His name was expunged from the file, as if he had never lived. It must have something to do with the hanging, mustn't it?

You mean the files were systematically edited
after the fact?

Files were tidied up, but more than this, during the chaos of the regime's collapse, when the secret service could not yet estimate what the consequences of these events would be, they were also destroyed. A whole lorryload of dossiers was tipped into a mountain ravine in the Carpathians – this is just one example of many.

When I went to Romania in 1990, there was no Securitate any more. The secret service had supposedly been disbanded. Today we know that, during this time, Securitate agents continued to receive their salaries and were then seamlessly transferred to the newly founded SRI – the Romanian Information Service. But back then, I simply walked into the secret service building in Timişoara unchallenged. I went down into the cellar, to see the prison cells which my friends had been locked up in. I also did this to convince myself that the Securitate really did no longer exist, not even down in that cellar. And I found the room where they used to photograph the prisoners. There were still tripods standing in there, and big cardboard boxes containing carefully sorted photos. Three pictures of the same face, always three – once from the front with eyes opened wide, and twice in profile from left and right, to capture the line of their nose, the tip of their chin and their ears. The same misery was visible in each of these faces. And in between the photos were the index cards containing the prisoners' personal information and fingerprints. I was looking through the photos and index cards when there was a clatter behind me. I flinched – my handbag had fallen from a shelf on to the floor. My heart was pounding in my head, I gasped for air and tried to convince myself that I felt no fear here any more – or no real fear at least, at most an imaginary one. In the past, I would have had my toothbrush in my handbag, because I thought I would have to go down to the cellar once my interrogation was over. Now there was no prison down here, just me and a fear without a cause. Without a cause, but as real as an iron bar in your throat. My handbag wasn't the same one I had used when I went to my interrogations, it didn't know the secret service and yet it seemed to me to be more alive in this cellar than I was. I felt as if this handbag were joining forces with my fear from back then to play tricks on me.

Everything there had been abandoned. I could have helped myself to those photographs, but which face would I have taken? And what for? I don't know why, but I didn't have the heart to do it. I felt queasy. I didn't go looking any further for the cells in the end because I didn't want to leave that one straight corridor; I didn't want to get lost in the labyrinth. I also wasn't sure whether someone had seen me enter the building after all and might come down after me. Instead I walked into a room, half of which was taken up by a huge oven bricked into one corner. An oven with thick loam walls, like our oven for baking bread in the village, just much bigger – the oven door was the size of a door to a room. It stood open, and there were several long fire pokers lying there. The oven was full, from top to bottom, of charred, curled paper: burnt files. I thought of my grandmother; our oven must have been just as full when the Russians came into our village. When, out of fear about their son's Nazi books, they spent three days burning his library.

In Romania, an ex-Securitate agent can have any job today. These people never disappeared, they helped themselves to government property thanks to their influence and position and became rich, arrogant 'democrats'. Up until now I have not heard a single one of them utter a word of regret about their earlier lives. There is no public discussion about the Securitate, the police or the border guards. Civil society has not asked them anything, not even about the murders.

After the fall of Ceauşescu, when I returned to Romania in the spring of 1990 I visited Timişoara and I bumped into my interrogator by chance, in the city centre. It was still cold, and he was wearing a karakul hat on his head. I wouldn't even have recognised him if he hadn't been so shocked: I had only ever seen him bareheaded in the office. He, however, had recognised me immediately, and forced his way as fast as he could into a queue for eggs in front of the nearest building. He knew that it was risky at the time to be recognised as a secret service agent by passers-by. People were still angry, they got involved when someone caught 'their' secret service agent on the boulevard – there were lynchings.

I followed him, stuffed my hands in my coat so they wouldn't tremble, and stood next to him in the queue. He turned his face away from me. I wanted to scream, but I had a bitter taste in my mouth, I couldn't think any more. What was it all for? I said, far too quietly. You see, now you have to be afraid of me. I couldn't speak any louder, my revulsion was so quiet. Then I walked away. Is there a rage that makes you quiet and empty and cowardly?

The worst thing was that, after all these years, even in this queue for eggs, I reflexively addressed him as '*Sie*', using the polite, formal 'you'.

The Regime Buries Its Crimes

As well as this friendship group in which reliance on one another was pushed to the utmost limit, there is a female friend who appears several times in your work. From the hard times in the factory onwards, she was your ally and you trusted her.

My friend Jenny was Romanian, she didn't speak a word of German. And she wasn't interested in literature. Or politics. She was an engineer specialising in welding technology, but I never detected an interest in welding technology in her either. She was very intelligent, she could have studied anything. How she came to welding I don't know. I never asked her; her job never occurred to me when we were together, she never said a word about it. But her profession wasn't a good fit for her or for the factory, I don't think there was anything at all that needed to be welded in there. She sat in a big office full of drawing boards and draughtsmen. She herself had no drawing board, just a rather empty desk.

Jenny was a unique apparition in this factory – she talked a lot, and fast. And what she said was quirky, cheeky and impulsive. She didn't listen out for words like I did, but her use of language was sensual, saucy, without ever tipping into vulgarity. Whatever she was saying, her sentences were, without her willing it, beautiful, full of images. She believed herself to be apolitical, but this was not the case. She didn't develop any big theories based on what she saw going on around her, but because she was so spontaneous she had a kind of innate intransigence. Her sensuality made her instinctively resistant to the grey oppression of the regime – she was incorruptible. She mocked the tinny Party speak, the meeting rituals, the hypocrisy and obtuseness of our bosses. Her patience wore thin during meetings, she couldn't stand the hours of 'stupidly sitting there until your arse is square' – as she called this wasted time. So she would stand up – without first indicating her intention to speak by raising her hand – and, very loudly and without any connection to what had just been discussed, say something untoward to the committee: I've been feeling hungry for hours. Or she would address the speaker as comrade so-and-so and then ask him what time it was. This wasn't directly political, but it was ambiguous – facetious and wicked, plaintive and ironic. Because her father had been a high-ranking Party member in the factory in days gone by, the bosses put up with it. I always had in the back of my mind that Jenny came from the *nomenklatura*. But why would I hold that against her? I couldn't help having an SS father, and she couldn't help having a Communist one. And she didn't belong to the *nomenklatura* mentally, unlike the two ladies from the records office.

Jenny and I had absolutely nothing in common. But affinity can of course develop in entirely different ways. It may be a slower process – because you look at each other wide-eyed, and marvel at each other precisely because you are so different. Nor did I ever get the impression, in all those years, that we were growing any more similar. Our differences remained the same, while we grew incrementally closer. I believe we developed this great friendship because our differences were exactly what each of us needed. For me, Jenny represented a necessary sheering off from my circle of friends – a need to not talk about literature or politics, but about other topics. About small, trivial things. They had no urgency; I could pick and choose them myself. And they were important for this reason alone. They had – and this was the best thing about them – nothing to do with the dictatorship. They never became dominant and dark like my fear. Because in our group, we were already beholden to each other and hardened, such that we could not encounter lightness. Even when we were larking around, descending into orgiastic laughter, the hilarity was edgy and it remained political. I so enjoyed being with my friends and wanted to be like them. And I behaved in this way in the group, too. But I also needed to be different, and this was only possible by sheering away from them. In order to endure the hopelessness, the seriousness, I needed the supposedly trivial, so-called 'women's business'.

I was fixated on clothes. I would spend whole half-days with Jenny at the seamstress's in the suburbs. First we would discuss designs, and then the patterns would be drawn. Then we had to show up for two or three fittings. I would often think of my aunt – of the stuffed white owl, of her father and the mulberry tree – and how I was allowed to go through her workshop picking up her sewing pins with a magnet. And on Sundays I would go to the flea market with Jenny to search for buttons: Bakelite, horn, thread or mother-of-pearl.

And we would take trips through the parks and to the edge of the city, where the weeds blossomed. We'd steal flowers, tie them into big bouquets. We'd pluck the white balls of blossom from the water clover and plait wreaths in such a way that the density of the flowers always remained the same. In such a way that the flower stalks bent but didn't break and were so delicately woven on the underside that you couldn't see the knots. Jenny's hands were clumsy, she was a stylish child of the city. As for me, my fingers seemed to have their own memory; my hands behaved as if they belonged once more to the village child in the river valley. On the edge of the city, the grasses were garish and swaying, but the thought that the Earth would gobble us up didn't come to my mind as I was plucking them. It seemed to me that we were able to scare away the State with these plucked weeds.

What exactly did Jenny know about your background, what did she know about your opinions, your literature, your friends?

Jenny knew that I wrote in German and that what I wrote was supposedly literature. But she didn't care about this. We never talked about writing. But she knew from the start, even before the harassment in the factory began, that I was very friendly with a group of writers. That my friends were all deemed to be enemies of the State, had experienced house searches and interrogations, that some of them had even been under house arrest or in prison. At the beginning, I merely had to make it clear to her what my position was. But then, the greater the daily threat grew in the factory, the more I kept having to tell her about it.

Before she knew me she had been sheltered, having been born into the *nomenklatura*. She had not had to distort herself in order to conform, and she had never needed to give any thought to how other people were faring. She knew about the repression that was going on, but only as hearsay. Political persecution happened, but to entirely different people – she didn't care about it. But she didn't care that she belonged to the *nomenklatura* either. If anything, it made her feel rather uncomfortable. I think that what happened to me in the factory politicised her. The defamation, my impotence and the absurdity of it all, the false game we played every day, and that I was entirely at the mercy of. That the State could do such a thing was incomprehensible to her. She never reacted with political statements, she always relied on physical action. Her curses were the most beautiful, because the force of her words was combined with her elegant gestures and sad eyes.

Her physical indignation was something you could rely on. Jenny didn't leave me alone. Everyone else in the factory avoided me, but she made a public display of our friendship: she sat down next to me on the staircase and ate with me. There was no dissidence in there, really, but her moral values resisted her environment. You needed a lot of self-confidence to do this.

I was never allowed to bring Jenny home with me, my circle of friends were suspicious of her. Her father was high up in the Party after all, and she had nothing to do with literature or politics, had no idea of our problems, and her behaviour was clueless and superficial, they said. I was being irresponsible; I might be enabling her to spy on me. And ultimately this was not something that only affected me. My friendship with this person had introduced a shard of uncertainty into our circle. I could feel that this wasn't true, that these were prejudices. I could feel that I wasn't risking anything, but I couldn't prove it.

At the group's request, I kept Jenny out of our circle of friends. I don't know whether she could sense why. Although I often spoke about our group, she never expressed an interest in getting to know them better – but I found having to maintain this distance between her and my other friends difficult. I felt dishonest both towards the group and towards Jenny. I couldn't tell the group how much I needed the lightness of my time with Jenny, and I couldn't tell Jenny that the group was avoiding her. Our group was bound together irrevocably, but my bond with Jenny was similarly irreversible. Every day, they belonged together and at the same time they were separate from each other. I think that the heart-beast crouches in these nests of feelings.

You didn't lose touch after you were dismissed from the factory either . . . Jenny stayed by your side, even though some people found this friendship suspect.

Jenny lived with her parents. Even after my dismissal from the factory, we saw each other almost every day. Most of the time we would meet in the city, as her father didn't want me to come into his house. He told me to my face that I was dangerous and the worst possible company for his daughter. This was not the last house that I would no longer be allowed to enter.

After I was thrown out of the factory, I urgently needed money. Jenny arranged for me to tutor for various families. I would take the children to school, pick them up, do homework with them or give them German lessons. But it didn't last long: soon the Securitate would appear wherever I was teaching and threaten the families, telling them that associating with me would have consequences. All of them obeyed and said I shouldn't come any more. It was normal. But it surprised me when they were open with me about their real reasons for letting me go: you're harming our family, you know, we don't do politics. Or: we can't ruin our child's future. Most of them invented salary cuts, or ballet or piano lessons which were supposedly more important for the child.

When visiting the students I tutored longest, for almost three months, I went to a fur house. The entrance hall was lined waist-high with fur, and the floors were covered with fur carpets. On the bureau, on the mirror table, lay fur throws of all colours: silver-grey, blue-black, copper-red and pale as old snow. They were long- and short-haired, smooth and curly. And it was the same in all the rooms, there was fur in the display cabinets, on the furniture. The mother and both sons wore slippers made out of fur. At their request, I would take off my shoes in the entrance hall and slip into my furry guest slippers. The bench in the kitchen was also covered in fur, even the oven gloves were made of fur.

The man of the house was a supervisor in the fur factory; 'a fur master', as his wife put it. I helped their sons with their homework. At first the fur master paid me as agreed, with money. Then with slightly less money and a pair of fur gloves. Then with just a bag of fur hats. I couldn't go on like this. I said: you can't eat fur; I need the money. Was *I* supposed to turn the fur hats into money? The Securitate would have been delighted, it would at last have justified their allegations of bootlegging. Besides, I was working for this family during the spring and summer! But even if it had been winter, you still couldn't eat fur. The fur master's house always smelt of freshly baked cakes, of vanilla and sugar and of moth powder. Once I dreamt that I was on my way home from tutoring the sons and felt fur between my toes and in the hollows of my knees and on my elbows, and that when I sat down on a bench I tried to rub the fur off, but that I couldn't because the fur had grown into my skin. The dream didn't entirely surprise me; I spent three to four hours at a time with the children. To me, the flat looked like a huge animal made of stolen fur. I know rationally that there's no connection whatsoever, but this fur house felt like an overture for my cut-up fox. As if there were two fur periods: first, the time of stolen fur, then the time of cut-up fur.

I also experienced two periods marked by the fear of death – or rather by two different fears of death, each independent of the other. My fear of death came from the secret service. And when I left the country, I brought this fear of death with me to Germany, because the threat didn't stop when I left Romania. But once I had left the country, another fear of death alighted on Jenny: that of fatal illness. She had cancer. This was a fear of death which did not allow for any relief. It was the terrible knowledge that her body itself had decided on death, that there was no way out of it, that there wasn't even a way round it.

Jenny was allowed to travel to Berlin to see you – however, she was given the assignment of spying on you. Her illness had made her vulnerable to blackmail. You describe your friend's visit and her

*confession that she was travelling by order of the secret
service. When you found a copy of your front-door key
in her suitcase, you threw her out.*

She had late-stage cancer. Mastectomy, chemotherapy:
she had done it all by this point. She was so young, only
in her mid-thirties, and she didn't have much time left.
She wanted to see me one final time. But that wasn't all. It
wasn't just a longing for me that brought her to Berlin, she
also had this much greater hunger for life. And then came
her betrayal.

I was so happy when she called and said that she had her
passport, that she was allowed to visit me.

And then she was actually there, sitting with me at my
table in Berlin, in my kitchen. And I was mad with happiness, raising both arms above my head and waving them in
the air as I cried: show me your passport! She rummaged
around awkwardly in her handbag but claimed she couldn't
find it, and left the bag standing wide open on the floor.
I could see the passport, I said there it is, and stretched
out my hand towards it. And then I saw the visas for all
sorts of countries: France, Italy and, when I leafed through
it some more, Spain and Greece. You didn't get passports
like that in Romania. I had to ask: what did you do to get
these?

She had an assignment to carry out. It would have been
pointless for her to lie. She had been asked to inform me
that I would end up on the kill list if I didn't stop insult-
ing Ceauşescu. That the whole operation had already been
planned in Bucharest, and that the Ministry would not
hesitate to have it executed if I continued. I had indeed
said, in an interview with *Spiegel* magazine just after my

arrival in Germany, that Ceauşescu had only been to school for four years, that he was illiterate, that he stuttered and that his speech was full of grammatical errors. But Jenny hadn't only been sent to warn me. What she didn't tell me at the time was that she had also been ordered to scrutinise my behaviour, to find out what cosmetic products and food I used, and make a duplicate of my front-door key. These were no less than preparations for the murder that she was supposedly warning me about. But on the night of her arrival in Berlin, she promised me that she would tell the Securitate a story that we would agree on together before she went back. That she could never do anything to harm me. I was distraught, but I believed every word she said. I was convinced that we would discuss everything and that she would stick to the story when she arrived back in Romania – I believed that she was clever enough to dupe the secret service. But then, when I found the duplicate key in her suitcase, everything came tumbling down.

With the key in my hand, I screamed that she was betraying me. She couldn't argue with me, nor did she even try. She was silent and stubborn – it was as if a door had closed between us. Quietly and confidently, she packed her suitcase, with no word of regret, as if everything that had happened between us were normal.

For whole days after she left, I could think about nothing other than how much I liked her and how much I needed to get rid of her. Did her cold self-assertion, her indifference to her betrayal come from her fatal illness? Had her life been reduced to what she could still achieve and what she would never have? Did she already carry within her this divided gaze: viewing the world from both this side of life and the beyond?

It got even worse: I discovered that Jenny was involved with the second-highest-ranking officer of the Timişoara Securitate.

She had lied to me and told me that her boyfriend was a lawyer, that he had just made a leap forward in his career and that nobody could know that she was involved with him because he was married. But I had met this man, and knew what he really was. Shortly before my departure for Germany, there was a final house search. Again, disguised as a break-in. The door had been forced open, and when I arrived home, as was typical, the police and my neighbours were already there. They were compiling a report saying that there was a radio or something like that missing, some sort of object, so that the break-in would seem plausible. I already had my passport and so I said: I thought I'd paid my dues. The policeman was young, attractive, well dressed – not the picture-book spy in a leather coat, plastic socks and a karakul hat. He said they had taken fingerprints – there was a poison-green powder dabbed all over the door – and that I should check what was missing in the flat. And, without looking, I said: nothing is missing. You're staging yet another burglary. You're from the secret service. Go to your office and take your colleagues' fingerprints, I said, because I know the game you're playing here, I've known it for years, I just thought it was finally over. I'm just waiting to leave. In ten days or in two weeks we'll be out of the country. I thought this meant that we had settled everything that needed settling. And then he showed me his ID: Criminal Investigation Department. Oh stop it, I said. You have all kinds of ID, whatever credentials you need. If you want to be a baker or an engineer or a chemist, you have all the relevant paperwork. I don't believe your ID at all.

But while 'Criminal Investigation Department' was a lie, the name on the ID wasn't. He would later become Jenny's lover.

And after the fall of the dictatorship, when I returned to Romania for the first time, I was once again faced with this egregious situation. I decided to visit Jenny, to talk everything through, and I found out that the Securitate officer was still her lover. That he was sitting in prison for having been involved in mass shootings during the revolution. That she visited him and stood by him, still. Jenny told me he was the most sensitive person she had ever met. It was like she'd been brainwashed. I slammed the door of her flat behind me and wandered through streets that were still strewn with wreaths for the dead. It was the second time that we had argued before parting ways. And it was the last time we saw each other. Shortly afterwards, Jenny died.

Twenty years later, Jenny's Securitate agent, like so many others, carved out a second career for himself – he became a regional manager for an Austrian insurance company. In an interview he boasted about having installed the bugs in my flat. And he said the Securitate had earned half of my Nobel Prize. After all, I had them to thank for the topics I had written about.

Did you ask yourself whether your relationship with Jenny had actually been a friendship, or if it was an assignment from the start?

I was very afraid of that. But when I was able to read my Securitate file at last, it turned out that the Securitate hadn't been interested in Jenny at first.

Despite being friends with me, she wasn't importuned until I left the country. Maybe this was because she had studied welding technology, wasn't interested in literature and didn't have any idea what I was reading or writing about, because she didn't speak a word of German. Or maybe she was simply under her father's protection at that time.

The secret service was a brisk, autocratic, narrow-minded men's club. Women were viewed as weak, silly and sentimental. They underestimated our friendship; it was probably classified as harmless 'women's business'. I suppose we were at least lucky on that front.

You write about a tangle of love and betrayal
which cannot be unsnarled.

If Jenny had said before her death that I should come to her again, I would have visited her once more. But she didn't want me to. And I couldn't visit her against her will. I wouldn't have been able to bear the imbalance in our relationship. Me, sitting there healthy, while she lay dying. Her greatest misfortune, her illness, was taken advantage of by the secret service. It was a form of torture. You cannot decide that you no longer like a person who has been so abjectly taken advantage of. But still, I had to forbid myself this friendship for my own protection. I could never do anything to harm you: she'd said these words to me in my kitchen in Berlin. I kept turning them over in my mind. Did she really believe that she wasn't causing me harm by duplicating my key for the secret service? Had she been driven by a desperate lust for life now that she had no future, only a rapidly diminishing present? Was she in denial about the consequences of her assignment? Or was it clear to her that she was leaving the land of friendship for that of betrayal? And was betrayal not tiring? Did she go on this journey for herself? Was it an attempt to live her short life to the full? Or was it a token of love for the secret service man, whom she never distanced herself from, even when he was sitting in prison for mass murder? Did she no longer think any action through to its logical end? Or, conversely: had she thought everything through to its end, even me?

When I next returned to Romania, after her death, I went to the graveyard where she was buried. I smoked a cigarette there and then left again. I wondered whether her lover ever visited her grave. He had long been released from prison, like all the Securitate agents, supposedly for lack of evidence. How helpless we are before a grave. I have never understood people who visit graveyards as though they were parks. They go for a walk or sit on a bench and read and marvel at the beauty of the gravestones. Every grave-yard is haunting to me, because I always imagine the dead people who are under the earth. I can't think it away. I'm not in a garden or a park. I know that I am *literally* walking over dead bodies – not as a figure of speech, but in actuality.

Even early on, you did not experience the graveyard as a calm place, but rather as one that was frighteningly alive.

Even as a child I found the graveyard uncanny. I had to water the flowers, alone or with other children, in the evening. Children have dark imaginations, and children without fairy-tale books make up the fairytales themselves.

Often it was very hot during the day, around forty degrees in the sun, and the graveyard was barren. There wasn't a single tree, just rows of graves, rank and file, like houses in a village, everything symmetrical. And then, when smoke came out of the graves in the gloaming . . . As a child, you hear that you have to cover the mirror so that the Devil doesn't snatch your soul, so you believe that the dead take their souls with them. They are with them in the coffin, but in the evening they come out. And you knew many of these dead people, so that in many cases you knew exactly what kind of soul you were dealing with. I saw all sorts of things in that graveyard: animals, objects . . . At the back of it was the pond with the frogs. They would sing their subterranean song, and they would plop into the water from the grassy bank because they would get startled when you came along with a watering can and disturbed the plants – the reeds would tower over me, swaying round my head, black and green in the night. All Hallows' Day also ignited the imagination, with its scent of candles and the way the wax would trickle down them forming knots, noses and strings – monstrous white figures of horror.

I've always felt there was something dangerous about graveyards, because you can no longer see what is beneath your feet – it's like standing in tall grass. And in Catholic graveyards you also have photos on the gravestones, which is particularly macabre. They gaze at you, these round gravestone portraits. I can never leave a graveyard still feeling light inside. I can never visit one and simply say: what beautiful flowers. No, instead I have often thought: the roots have taken the dead, and now they are blossoming; this is a monstrous world. And I know of another village where they referred to the graveyard well as 'gobwater', because the groundwater ran through the moustaches of the dead. Nobody was cremated in the village graveyard. Each person's body lay intact under the earth in a coffin, and I knew that they were lying down there and were watching me through the soles of my feet.

In graveyards, I'm also afraid of Death – that it might catch you if you get too close to it, that it might notice you and wonder whether it shouldn't try its luck. And if there is somebody you were close to buried in the graveyard, then you are also close to their death, of course.

The high grass, the hungry grasses, appeared again later, in connection with the 'Paupers' Graveyard'. This, however, was not just a graveyard for paupers, but also for the victims of the secret service. You didn't want to talk about it at first, because you were afraid that nobody in the West would believe you . . .

The Paupers' Graveyard in Timișoara was used to bury political offenders – to bury them on the one hand, and on the other to expose them. This is where the regime buried its crimes. In the case of many of the dead, we don't even know who they were. Some graves had wooden crosses, but most of them had nothing at all. You could only guess at the contours of the individual graves beneath the high grass. The dead were put into the earth without a coffin, as the State will have avoided incurring any extra expense – they just hastily buried them in shallow graves, and it didn't cost a thing.

The Paupers' Graveyard was in an ordinary, recently built neighbourhood and looked like a patch of wasteland, hidden behind a very high concrete wall in the middle of the city. You could go in and out as you liked; the entrance was a warped metal door. The graveyard was quite big – a wild, flowery, grassy landscape. You could see into it from the upper floors of the blocks of flats surrounding it.

And right in the middle of it stood a concrete lodge, and in the middle of this lodge was a concrete table. For a time, the body of a drowned person – a naked young woman with silt in her hair – was laid out on the concrete table. But she had not drowned by accident, she had been drowned. Her hands and feet were bound with wire. My heart rose up into my throat before this concrete table; I thought of my 'blond visitor' in the factory. And two sentences ricocheted between my temples: 'we'll throw you in the river,' and 'whoever dresses cleanly cannot arrive in Heaven dirty.' In this woman, I saw the completion of the future he intended for me.

The lodge contained a single small, monstrous room with a water tap coming out of the wall and only a narrow opening as an entrance, there was no door. On the outer wall, someone had written '*vampiraş*' in red paint – little vampire.

We searched this graveyard for the grave of the man who was supposedly responsible for one of the staged break-ins at our flat. He had already been in prison – who knows what for – when they pinned this break-in on him. And then we were told that there would be no trial, because the burglar had died in prison. Supposedly, his name was 'Seracu' – which in Romanian means 'the pauper'. We asked after his relatives, and they said he had nobody. His name led us to the Paupers' Graveyard. We did actually find a grave with a wooden cross bearing this name. And on this grave, on that hot day, lay fresh flowers.

What does one do with such a place after the dictator-ship has fallen? In Romania, they did nothing at all. The concrete lodge still stands there, just as it did back then, with the word '*vampiraş*' still written on it.

Two Sighs of Relief

*After the fall of the dictatorship, you requested
your secret service file, but you didn't gain access
to it for a long time.*

I only gained access to it in 2008, ten years after the foundation of the Romanian National Council for the Study of the Securitate Archives, which itself was only founded ten years after the fall of the dictatorship. And during these two decades, the files remained in the hands of the newly founded secret service, the SRI. If the Council wanted to review a file, it first had to request it from the SRI, which was largely staffed by old Securitate agents – who of course took a good look at the file before releasing it. Or they wouldn't release it at all and would instead tell you the file was still 'being processed'.

As I have already mentioned, the younger Securitate agents had been transferred seamlessly from the old security service into the SRI. In their new-old agency, the new-old agents gave themselves ten years to clean up the files that they themselves had compiled, and thus knew front to back.

At first, the Council informed me that there were no files left because the people had stormed the secret service building during the revolution and destroyed the files. Some time later, I was then sent twenty pages. These twenty pages, however, did not include a single concrete event that had anything to do with me. This file couldn't even be described as an act of deception, they hadn't even attempted to make it appear plausible – it was all just an astoundingly idiotic, barefaced lie, a display of the kind of arrogance I knew from the days of the interrogations.

Many years later, I did finally gain access to my full file, in two batches with a significant delay between them. But nothing about this record is complete. There are whole years missing, and the factory doesn't figure in it at all. You can glean from it the carousel of informers, of aliases, and the places, conversations, assessments, as well as the suggestions of plans to defame me. But the people who gave these orders are missing. The file does not mention a single full-time Securitate agent. I had hoped that it might reveal which agent had monitored Roland Kirsch at the end, that his letters to me, the last postcard before he died, might be included in my file, or at least that there would be copies of them, perhaps with comments in the margins. There had only been a short amount of time between his last postcard and his death. There were no 'coincidences' when it came to the delivery of post. The secret service thought very carefully about what post was delivered to you and what was suppressed, about when it was kept back and why. But the files are silent – even when it comes to those who died in the twilight between suicide or murder. If the Securitate didn't have anything to cover up, these documents could have been left in the files. The State could, if it was innocent, prove its innocence using these files. So why did it not do so?

But all the culprits, big or small, must be protected, and so they remain unnamed. One example is when the journalist Rolf Michaelis* visited from Hamburg. During the period when I wasn't allowed to travel, he wanted to come and see me in Timişoara – this was just after the publication of *Nadirs*. He sent me a telegram and he flew to Romania. But I wasn't home to welcome him, because his telegram never reached me. It was not until I was in Germany that he told me what had happened during this visit. It was winter, and public transport had been suspended in order to save fuel. A 'helpful' man in the hotel offered to drive him to my block of flats. There was no electricity at this time either, so the lift wasn't running and the staircase was dark, and he walked up to my flat on the fifth floor. When he rang my bell, three figures came out of the rubbish chute chamber and beat him up. They broke the toes on both his feet and left him lying in front of the door. He dragged himself down to the street, where to his astonishment the 'helpful' driver was still waiting. Back at the hotel, Michaelis packed his bags and flew home as fast as possible.

The intercepted telegram is also missing from my file, and of course there is not a word in there about Michaelis's visit or the assault. One wouldn't be able to hold anyone responsible based on the files alone.

Anyway, the files concerning the continued persecution of émigrés in the West are officially off-limits. In present-day Romania, these are still classified as state secrets. Why does

---

*   Rolf Michaelis (1933–2013) was a German journalist and author. At the time Herta Müller refers to here he was working for *Die Zeit*, one of the country's most politically and culturally influential weekly newspapers.

Romania not want to expose its former Securitate agents abroad? Does it still need them? Have they now been given new assignments? I certainly hope they're not still working on the same ones. There are scores of murdered Romanian émigrés, but no convicted offenders. Why does present-day Romania feel obliged to protect the murderers? It's possible that they never left, but have been living among us in the West to this day.

So far, no Romanian government has taken any steps to shed light on the Securitate's crimes. I once received a summons from the Security Agency in Berlin because a Romanian agent had been arrested on suspicion of having been contracted to carry out murders in Germany, and the police had found my address in his notes. I knew his face from somewhere, but I told the police that I had never seen him before, because after the vile suspicions directed at me in the reception centre in Nuremberg I never wanted to have anything to do with the services again – I could no longer trust them, even if trusting them would work in my favour. Only the files of the Romanian secret service could have shed light on this case – and without such cases being cleared up, one is always going to be left feeling wretched.

Did you make any surprising discoveries in the files? Were any friends or anyone you were intimate with informers for the Securitate? The recruitment of friends, sometimes even spouses, was an important instrument for the secret service.

This was probably their intention when they tried to recruit me at the factory. They hadn't reckoned with me refusing, even in the face of their threat to have me dismissed. They probably did want me to spy in the factory, but they mainly wanted me to infiltrate the city's artistic milieu and, above all, my circle of friends. This is the only way I can explain my 'blond visitor'. Thanks to other Romanian writers, I knew that he was working with the literature bureau. At the time, I couldn't imagine that the secret service could infiltrate such close, intimate relationships, using people you trusted. After all, this could only happen by poisoning the tightest of bonds. The Stasi called this 'disintegration': a macabre word and an important term in their daily business. Disintegrating sounds like decomposing, evokes total annihilation. And this term is not even an exaggeration, it is commensurate with the calamity that was wreaked by this poisoning.

After studying my file, I was able to breathe two sighs of relief.

First: my friendship with Jenny was real. The secret service only came into play right at the end.

Second: there was no informer in our circle of friends.

The Securitate did not manage to flip even one of us; they failed to poison our friendship. Both individually and as a group, we were comprehensively spied on, but only from the outside – by neighbours, colleagues, acquaintances, journalists. It was no surprise to see this in my file. But I was appalled by how thoroughly they had bugged our flat, that they were listening in on all our rooms, on everything we did at home, both day and night. The secret service probably decided to do this because they could not infiltrate our circle of friends – and the trouble they went to is astonishing. For they didn't just conceal the bugs. In order to install them, they drilled both through the ceiling of the flat beneath ours and through our flooring. The bugs in our flat were wired to the flat underneath us. We were often flabbergasted by how much the secret service knew and asked us about during interrogations. We had no telephone, so they couldn't be wiretapping us – instead, we thought the information came from directional microphones. They must occasionally be working outside on the street, we thought, listening in on us through the closed windows of parked cars or from apartments on the same floor as ours in other blocks of flats nearby. This was how we explained to ourselves how the Securitate inexplicably knew so much. Despite the constant harassment, none of us thought that we ranked so high in their list of enemies of the State. We were also all clueless technologically, so we grossly underestimated the Securitate's equipment. We thought they used technology from the Stone Age, along with everyone else in our immiserated country.

And the second big shock I got while reading my file was the doggedness and infamy with which the Securitate pushed to discredit me in Germany. The defamation in the factory was just the beginning. After I was dismissed, the Securitate drew up and implemented dozens of plans and methods, all 'measures for disinformation' about me.

If people in the West thought you were a spy, then everything you said or wrote about the dictatorship would lose credibility. Was this the plan?

Before I got hold of my file, I thought I had been allowed to travel to the West to pick up my literary prizes, to help show that Romania was not as restrictive as the West claimed. But this was a naive theory. The literary prizes were only of secondary importance. The main reason for my travel was an entirely different one: to permanently discredit me in the West as an opponent of the regime and as a victim of political persecution, and to invalidate the contents of my books and any public criticism of the regime too. The secret service hoped, assumed in fact, that I would stay in Germany. They wanted me out of Romania. And, thanks to their disinformation, I was supposed to be so compromised in Germany that no one would believe me any more, regardless of what I said or wrote. The plan was clever, and truly vile – it was diabolical. The logic went: if the rumour that I was an agent was seen as credible, and if, in parallel, I myself appeared in the West, it would push this rumour beyond doubt, since no one was allowed to travel, apart from those who profited from the regime. In order to spread this rumour, letters denouncing me as an agent were sent to the editorial departments of German television channels, radio stations and newspapers. The letters were drafted by the Securitate. Then, Romanians who had been sent abroad, as part of a folklore group for example, were given the task of throwing the letters, now rewritten in their own handwriting, into postboxes in the West.

On top of this, there were also the actions of the Banat Swabians, who accused me of having written *Nadirs* by order of the Securitate, and of disparaging the 'Germanness' of their minority. Supposedly, my trips to the West were a reward for having done this. In Southern Germany, a troop of these 'compatriots' came along to several of my readings with orders to disrupt them. They would stamp their feet, jeer and shout. And so some of my readings had to be cut short. But I had no idea how directly the rage of this 'delegation of Swabians' was connected to the

Securitate. Only when I accessed my file was I able to see that there were Securitate agents among the leadership of the *Landsmannschaft*. And that the *Landsmannschaft* used its influence with broadcasting commissions to harass the editors who had interviewed me.

I have never, to this day, understood how the *Landsmannschaft* could continue not to care about the dictatorship in Romania for all those years. As if their homeland were located in a picture book and not in an authoritarian state. Villages and red poppies, folk music and traditional costumes, customs and traditions were the stuff of their homeland. But these are precisely the things that the dictatorship destroyed. The villages were left empty, and everyone abandoned three hundred years of history. In these villages that had been tortured by Socialism, one's sense of home had metamorphosed into a suitcase. What use is a home you cannot live in? The *Landsmannschaft* never said a word about that.

In 2009, during some research, an academic discovered Oskar Pastior's Securitate file. Pastior had been forced to work for the secret service shortly after returning from a labour camp. He told the German authorities about this when he entered the country, but then kept quiet about it for decades – it was only revealed after his death. If he were still alive today, you've said that you would tell him to write about it. What questions would you have had for him?

I would have wanted to know exactly how his recruitment happened. In a note that we found after Pastior's death, he'd written the word 'kidnapping' underneath the heading 'Attempted Reconstruction'. This word horrifies me. Pastior always considered each word very carefully, not just when he was writing but also in conversation. He never exaggerated, he was always restrained in the way he formulated things. But this note says 'kidnapping'. I have to imagine something bad here. Did they put him in a car? Threaten him out in the open, or lock him up inside a room? We know that there were many clandestine locations – extorted flats in private residential blocks, hotel rooms, sheds, isolated buildings of all kinds – forming a labyrinth of fear in which the Securitate could blackmail and torture freely. I have already mentioned how they drove Rolf Bossert out to a patch of woodland. Pastior's kidnapping, however, took place fifty years earlier – back then the Securitate's methods were even more brutal.

We know from Pastior's file that he was forced to choose between collaboration and prison. After five years in the labour camp, where he had seen so many internees starve and freeze to death, he signed his declaration of commitment because, having only just been set free, he did not want to return to prison again. And at that time, you never heard of a sentence of less than ten years. He was bound by that signature for ten years, and it tortured him until he was finally able to leave Romania. In the note, he also writes that he had regular migraines. When you know how scrupulous Pastior was, you can imagine what a profound break this must have been for him. A complete loss of self-respect, and terrible feelings of guilt. He calls his forced collaboration his 'revulsion complex'.

After he survived the camp, he ended up in the Securitate's sights because of some poems he'd written while he was interned. They were deemed to be 'anti-Soviet agitation'. They had locked him up for five years in a Soviet camp and now they wanted to lock him up again in prison because of seven labour camp poems . . . Isn't it tragic? To be robbed even of your own survival.

Pastior was never able to get out of this commitment: he couldn't break free from this signature. But he did try to resist. He wrote reports very rarely – not even once a year. And his reports are trivial. I don't believe a single one was written on his own initiative. I have seen many other files and I am surprised that the Securitate tolerated Pastior's negligence. It bordered on ineptitude. And I wonder what price he paid for this passivity.

On top of this, there is also Pastior's homosexuality. This too could land you in prison, and so he also had to hide his private life. It could be used to blackmail him. And he had to ensure his family never heard anything about it. Along with the State and the people in the small town he came from, Pastior's family would not have had any understanding for it. He was afraid they might disown him. After he had returned from the labour camp, his mother and grandmother would often ask him: don't you have a girlfriend yet? From the point of view of both the State and the family, any alternative to being in a heterosexual relationship was unthinkable. Oskar Pastior spoke to me at length about his hidden homosexuality and the additional loneliness he felt in the labour camp as a result; about homosexual encounters in his small town and later in Bucharest; about the fear that went around when people you knew were picked up and arrested. He told me how you had to be prepared for the possibility that you might be next, because the person who had been arrested might have cracked during their interrogation.

Oskar Pastior remained in the claws of the regime until 1968, when he was able to stay on in the West at the end of his first trip abroad. He was a person robbed of his own life, who was fair game for the State and forced to be an informer through threats of violence. Someone who had been forced to collaborate with the Securitate; a forced labourer once more. In his 'Attempted Reconstruction' note, he describes himself as having 'become innocently guilty'. And that is exactly how I see it, not because he said it about himself, but because I have read the seven reports in his files.

Before reading Pastior's file, you reacted very severely
– partly because you had been so close to him.

When, after his death, I heard about his collaboration, I was appalled. I couldn't imagine him as an informer. His involvement with the Securitate had taken place forty years earlier, and I thought that perhaps back then, when he was a young man and constantly surrounded by fear, he had been an entirely different person. Before Pastior's death, you could not yet access any files in Romania.

In my initial fury I was disgusted that, despite our close relationship – and despite all our long discussions about the internal states that were created by the camp, about coercion and the end of vanity and dignity – Pastior had never uttered the word 'Securitate'.

I kept asking myself how someone could keep silent when they were such a close friend. I couldn't understand it. But somehow it could be done. I think for a start he was very afraid of my experience with the secret service. And he was even more afraid for us, for our friendship. And within this friendship, he was more afraid for himself than for me. And he was right to be. However he had portrayed to me the circumstances of his signing that declaration of commitment, and the ten years that had followed, I would not have been prepared to believe how innocently he had become guilty. Nor how little he had reported over the course of those ten years. I would have rejected his explanations. I would have been convinced that he was playing things down, making excuses for himself.

In order to protect himself, Pastior had to make hiding his second nature. For years, his impotence taught him not just how to carry more than his own load, but also how to keep quiet while doing so. He felt disgrace keenly, and he believed this secret was disgraceful. And he was right. I would definitely have terminated our friendship, had he made such a confession. And this would have shattered him once more. And then I would be reproaching myself today, but it would be too late, because I would not have found out the truth until seeing his file after his death.

After Oskar Pastior's death, it seemed to me that he had lived his life on tiptoes. He always carried within him a thoughtfulness so great that he was almost too self-aware. He treated everyone and everything so circumspectly. It is no accident that he called his note 'Attempted Reconstruction'. After his survival, a timidity took shape at the centre of the person named Oskar Pastior, and from that point on he regarded most of his days as no more than attempts at life. For him, freedom was encased within what appeared to be compulsive behaviours. For example, he always led with his right foot when he stepped over a threshold: when he got into a car, or got out of a lift. And this was no foolish game, it was a necessity. These strategies put into practice internal principles on which everything depended. Freedom, for

Oskar, was an act of redefining compulsion. As to whether it was possible to be successful in such an endeavour – on that point, Pastior was inscrutable. He spoke of the 'merciful compeller' in life as in writing:

'In me sits the merciful compeller, a relative of
the hunger angel. [. . .] He climbs into my brain,
pushing me into the enchantment of compulsion,
because I am afraid of being free.'

Life, for Pastior, was unique, but the constituent parts of this unique piece were repeated chains of events. And each chain had its own rules. I think that for Pastior, freedom didn't look like breaking a rule, but rather overburdening it, until it could no longer hold – and so could no longer dictate anything to him, could no longer determine his existence.

The Wonders of My Fatherland

Nineteen eighty-four was an important year for you.
Nadirs *was published by the Berlin-based Rotbuch*
Verlag, you won the Aspekte *Literature Prize for the*
best literary debut of the year, as well as the Rauris
Literature Prize, and suddenly you were allowed to
travel to Germany. Previously, you had not even been
allowed to visit Bulgaria or Hungary as a tourist.

I was allowed to travel to the West three times – on each
occasion I was there to receive a literary prize. Before that, I
had not been allowed to travel. I wanted to go to Klagenfurt
when I was nominated for the Ingeborg Bachmann Prize,
but I was not allowed to. At the time, I had had my submis-
sion for the prize smuggled into the West by someone from
the Goethe Institute. I couldn't even apply to travel back
then. To apply, either your place of employment or your
spouse had to provide a guarantee that you would come
back. I, however, having been chucked out of the factory,
had no place of employment – and, since I was divorced, I
didn't have a husband to vouch for me either. They refused
to even acknowledge receipt of my application to travel at
that point. But when *Nadirs* was published in Germany in

1984, the secret service decided to let me out of the country, and I was suddenly offered a position as a teacher, which meant I did now have a place of employment. And then the headmaster – despite the fact that he did not know me – issued me with the requisite certificate. I didn't know what had hit me.

On one visit I attended the Frankfurt Book Fair, and then returned home again as planned. My position as a teacher had already been filled by someone new, because they thought I would stay in Germany. This was awkward for the headmaster, as he had to let the newly hired teacher go again. He complained about this to me, in confidence: he couldn't understand how anyone could be so stupid. So many people risked their lives to get out, and I just came back – it beggared belief.

You weren't just in the West for a few days, but for weeks. What images did you return to your country with?

Upon my return, I went back to the school. The poor children were sitting in coats and gloves inside the classroom. It was winter, and nowhere in the country had any heating. But the absurd inspections of the children's hair length and their school uniforms at the school gate every morning continued. And every week there was 'pre-military training', with the children dressed in grotesque uniforms, with tassels and sashes and little stars signifying military ranks. And there was the head-shaving: because of scabies, because of lice, but also as punishment for any tiny infraction. And I returned to the intolerably dishonest meetings, to the dissembling and the opportunism of my colleagues.

I knew this world, of course, but now I could compare it to how things were when you were allowed to speak freely. When you did not have to constantly have two faces and contend with two reckonings for your actions: an external and an internal reckoning. Because if you had, just for a moment, actually said aloud what you thought in this school, you would immediately have gone to prison.

It was only when I was in the West that I understood how life had been stolen from us in Romania – that we were not just being robbed of our voices, but also of our lives. We had bad clothes, we had bad teeth, or no teeth, and no medicine. People died for the most trivial reasons and thought this was normal. They were worth nothing to the State. We had no aspirin and no cotton wool, there were no tampons, no sanitary towels, nothing. Women walked around with rags in their trousers.

And on top of this came the corruption and the bribery. Amid this scarcity, you could further humiliate and tame people by turning off their heating in the middle of winter and depriving them of basic foods, by forcing them to spend a whole day queuing for a loaf of bread and a bottle of milk.

We were only viewed as individuals when we were seen as enemies of the State.

Our whole life was censored. Censorship is not just about a sentence being struck through in a book – censorship was everything. All of this was really brought home to me in Germany. I've always thought that, in the West, respect for an individual is shown in the smallest things. Plasters for cuts or corns, tampons, cotton buds – these are all such banal things, but that's the point: they are not banal, and they are not just a commodity. If, like me, you come from an immiserated society, they have an entirely different value.

I would stare at the people on the U-Bahn like a child: they had such clean hands. There was so much to take in: the world was garish, everything was bright and the colours were restless. My eyes hurt. I came from the grey silence of dictatorship and poverty. Now adverts stared at me on every corner, bold and lively. I thought: this is what life looks like when you are allowed to think and say what you want. And this was overwhelming and almost impossible to bear. It made me happy, but it was also painful. I didn't dare rest in this happiness, I just felt distraught.

When I went to a restaurant in the evening for the first time in Frankfurt and saw the napkins, flowers and candles on the tables and looked through the menu, before I was even able to order anything the first thing I did was cry.

The differences between East and West often appear in your essays. On the one hand, the contrast allows you to see even more clearly how many varieties of injury a dictatorship can inflict on people – on the other hand, loping comfortably through life also risks making people thoughtless. 'They have their heads full of books, but not one of them has made even a detail of the absence of freedom comprehensible to them,' is your most acerbic way of formulating this point. You contrast this with what you call the 'foreign gaze'.

People have often said I have a foreign gaze, but they thought it was because of my migration from Romania to Germany, and the change from one country to another.

People interpret the foreign gaze geographically, but it

is not geographical, it is biographical, psychological. The foreign gaze is an internal thing, it doesn't stem from a change from one country to another, but rather from a loss of self-assurance. And I experienced this loss in Romania. I'd felt completely alienated for years – robbed and injured by the State – before I even thought of leaving the country. I already felt alienated when the entrails of beasts, lit up by the light inside the fridge at my hall of residence, became my heart-beast, or when the handkerchief became my staircase office in the factory, or when the corpse sugar from the lime trees covered the street, when I saw how my interrogator had fingernails like pumpkin seeds, or when the cut-up pelt in my bedroom mutated from a fox into a hunter.

The foreign gaze, to me, is a threatened gaze, it's looking in fear, feeling afraid of everything, including yourself. Then again, perhaps it is not just fear, but also feeling lost, because nothing is self-evident any more. Because you have to look too deeply into things, such that you become hopelessly mired in them. Because nothing runs smoothly in your day. You are too deeply involved in all things, always a fraction too submerged. And I brought all this with me from Romania.

You can't escape it, it is the injury you carry around with you. And added to this are your new surroundings. This new environment is not unpredictable, but you are. And then unexpected connections develop, making the harmless appear threatening. The tyranny of memory. You step on to a train and you see in your compartment an advert for a sleeper train, featuring a blonde woman in a white nightgown, and above the picture are the words: Inge Wenzel on the way to Rimini. And this white nightgown catapults you back to Romania. You were once on a sleeper train on the way to Bucharest, and there was a woman in a white nightgown with you on the top bunk in your compartment. And you spent the entirety of this nighttime journey afraid that the secret service might throw you off the train.

Why was Inge Wenzel wearing the same nightgown as the woman on the top bunk? Something jumps out of time. The present metamorphoses into what you are carrying inside your head. Something you had forgotten about is suddenly there again and you become so helpless. Visibly or invisibly, these things you bring with you keep being made present again. And if it hadn't been the nightgown, then perhaps the tyranny of memory would have transformed another object.

In Romania you had to constantly look out for yourself, you could only trust your friends. And then, suddenly, you found yourself in the limelight as a writer: you made public appearances, gave readings to large audiences. How did you experience this change of role?

One of the invitations I received was to the Rauris Literature Prize, to this small village, high up in the mountains, this world of rocks. The Grossglockner Mountain in the sky. It seemed to me as if the mountain had not grown from the bottom upwards but vice versa, that it did not so much have height as depth. It was hanging from the top downwards like a funnel of stone, as though it might suck up the whole village. And there was a smell of cow dung everywhere, which reignited my old village grief. But despite the smell, I didn't see a single cow. And I thought maybe the smell had been created especially for the tourists, using something like an air freshening spray – but one for wide, open spaces, rather than for freshening up rooms inside. I imagined that there were 'village sprays' in Austria, with mountain scents suggestive of Alpine cows and flowering meadows. Sprays were something entirely new to me anyway, especially air freshening sprays.

Readings in front of hundreds of people made me feel lonely inside. I was confronted with myself in a way that was different, more acute than if I had been alone. From Romania I knew only the loneliness of writing, the fear of house searches, the act of *hiding* my writing with people who would not arouse suspicion, or in Jenny's garden. My deep-seated fear of all interrogations resurfaced unexpectedly and against my will when I found myself standing in front of an audience, and it hurt me. My head would throb, because I knew the place where my writing came from and how different it was to where I found myself reading it out loud, and that this was an unauthorised meeting. I couldn't say any of this to anyone, because I didn't want to complain. I felt I should appear happy if people looked at me. They shouldn't see that I felt, from top to toe, as if my whole being were unauthorised.

Even though I was constantly impressed, amazed, even enthused by all these new things, I didn't dare feel happy. I wasn't free inside my head, I thought I wasn't entitled to happiness.

You spoke openly and very directly about the dictatorship on television and in newspaper interviews: you named the offences and crimes of the regime, even though you could safely assume that the authorities were monitoring this in Romania . . .

I did not want my travelling to come at the cost of silence. It was very important to me that people should find out what was happening in Romania. If I had wanted to stay silent, I might as well have stayed home. I wanted to travel, but I did not want to let myself be used by the regime, even if I knew that this attitude would create new problems for me when I went back. There were many people in Germany who tried to convince me to stay in the West. But, to me, there was no question that I had to return: I had promised my friends; I had promised myself. My staying in Germany was absolutely out of the question. I didn't want to hang anyone out to dry and I would not have been able to bear the thought that the State would take revenge on my friends. To put it tritely: I would not have found any peace in the West at that time. I would have felt guilty that others were paying the price for my decision. And there would have been no way for me to protect them.

So I went back every time. I had to hand in my passport within twenty-four hours of my return. At the passport office, the clerk would make a phone call, and I always knew what was going to happen next. The corridors between the passport office and the secret service were connected to one another, and within a minute my interrogator would appear. And then the 'analysis' of my trip would begin. They had collected everything: every broadcast, every newspaper article, my book reviews too. And I was confronted with them all and asked whether I really had said all of these things. I did not deny anything, out of principle. I said it's all me, even the commas are mine. This was a curious strategy; I don't think they were expecting it. Much as the response to *Nadirs* had taken them by surprise, as did the fact that I had been awarded prizes. Suddenly I was no longer anonymous, no longer the weak link in our group. They were in over their heads here. My success also made it clear that their smear campaign had not worked – a campaign I was entirely unaware of at the time. It was the prizes above all that protected me. Possibly my friends too.

My interrogator would always ask me who in the West was protecting me and how I had ended up garnering so much attention. He couldn't understand it. He assumed that I was collaborating with the German intelligence service. He couldn't imagine that a bookshop or a university, for example, would invite me to a reading without having been instructed to do so by the State. It was genuinely shocking how dumb the secret service was. My interrogator could not imagine freedom, it did not fit inside his pattern of thought. Anything that was outside the control of the State was incomputable to him. I tried to teach him that there were independent institutions in the West; as I did so, he grew ever more suspicious that I was working for the BND* and that I had been tasked with spreading Western propaganda. He was convinced that in the West the secret service also sat inside every institution and recruited people from the East by blackmailing them – it was the only reality he'd ever known.

After the third trip, my interrogator said that my Socialist fatherland had given me a chance but that I had been too dumb to take it. I had behaved treacherously and ungratefully, and now my travels were over. I could spend the next twenty years exploring the many wonders of my fatherland instead. After this interrogation I was dismissed

---

*   *Bundesnachrichtendienst* (BND), the West German foreign intelligence service.

from the school, and so I was unemployed once more. And my fee for the German edition of *Nadirs* went to the National Writers' Association, which needed foreign currency to finance the travel of State-sanctioned writers and literary officials. Instead, I received a voucher to spend at the 'shop'.* You couldn't buy any food there, only 'luxury products' such as soaps and deodorants that were available in any supermarket in Germany. My mother brought me meat and vegetables from the village every week – without her I would have starved.

Was it during this time that you took the decision to leave the country? Was it even a decision, or did everything push you towards it, so that ultimately this step was almost inevitable?

It was a decision, but one I made much later. I said for years that not everyone who opposed the regime could leave. Only one person should leave and then the others could stay. I didn't want to accept that Ceaușescu and his clan were occupying the whole country. The cruelty with which the regime pounced on us was monstrous. A quieter ideology that does not hinge on a cult of personality is awful enough – but this version of Romania, with its intense focus on Ceaușescu, was obscene. I couldn't bear it any more. I would turn on the television and see the face of this dictator, and every time it shook me and every time

---

*   'Shop' was the name used by Romanians to refer to stores where people could buy international goods in exchange for foreign currency; they were mainly used by members of the *nomenklatura*.

I would start to cry. I would stand at the bus stop and feel like I needed to scream. I would get on the bus and feel that I needed to loudly ask people how they managed to put up with it all. I had to force myself not to. I knew that I had reached a point where things could not go on for much longer, my nerves were so raw that I would soon snap. Was I willing to go to prison for that?

So I decided that I had to get out of there, if there was still time. I had been warned: Bossert had fled too late. The persecution had remained in his head; he was afraid of every police car in Germany, he tortured himself with hallucinations. He could no longer come to terms with life. While he was still in Romania, he had hacked at his beard with a pair of scissors: it was his first act of violence against himself. This was the image I had in my mind's eye when I decided to leave.

Sometimes I thought this insanity would soon collapse, and sometimes it felt like it would keep its hold on the country for evermore, and certainly would outlast me. I said 'sometimes and sometimes' just now, but really I thought both at the same time. Perhaps I thought something different in each temple and the two things didn't even strike me as contradictory. I asked myself what use freedom was to me if I had to wait until I had lost my mind for it.

Little by little, almost everyone in our circle of friends applied to leave the country. Romania, with its countless luckless tales of escape – everyone wanted to leave. But for the German minority there was this magic word: '*Familienzusammenführung*', 'family reunion'. Under this label, the State would sell Romanian Germans for a bounty, and would take in a handsome amount of foreign currency. And before they could leave, State officials would also extort hefty bribes out of the Romanian Germans for their passports. An informal emigration industry developed: a system made up of hidden, semi-legal offices where, if you paid a lot of money, you could edge further up the emigration list. Because there were no reliable rules, many families had to wait fifteen, even twenty years for their passports. Some had no money for bribes, others had coughed up and got themselves into huge amounts of debt and it still didn't help. But it wasn't just about money: the biggest house in the village was usually the best guarantee that you would get your passport quickly. The State would take possession of the house, which often meant that the local policeman or Party secretary had taken an interest in it at some point and was waiting impatiently for the person to emigrate.

Just as with everyone else in our group of friends, I wasn't looking to be reunited with any family; the categories in the forms had nothing to do with our reasons for wanting to emigrate. 'Family reunion' was simply a comparatively easy way out, based exclusively on your relatives, on your aunts and uncles in Germany. But in the small print of the forms, it said that your application would be invalid if you had not answered all questions accurately and truthfully. We crossed out these questions and in place of the answers each one of us wrote down an entirely different personal reason for emigrating: persecution by the secret service, interrogations, house searches, dismissal from the factory, dismissal from several schools on grounds of individualism and lack of a Socialist conscience, censorship and publication bans and so on. Then we handed in the forms. We were ready for anything: for the forms to be declared invalid; for them to be perceived as a provocation and for us to be dragged into court because of them; for them to not care and instead let us emigrate because they wanted to get rid of us. I knew the latter response from my interrogations: off you go to your capitalist swamp, that's where you belong anyway.

There was no outraged reaction to the forms, though. There was no reaction at all. And instead the harassment continued. To keep me in a state of uncertainty, my application to emigrate was ignored at first. Then after a few months it emerged that the forms had been accepted. And after a mere one and a half years, Richard Wagner (to whom I was by then married) and I received the news that we were allowed to emigrate. And after that, our other friends received the same news. They wanted to get rid of us all, the whole group. Only Roland Kirsch, the youngest among us, said he wanted to stay a while longer, and that he would come later. We all know how that ended. Two years later he was found hanged. His last card read: 'Sometimes I have to bite myself on the finger to feel that I still exist.'

*One and a half years of waiting must have
strained your nerves. How does one live on
with 'time standing still'?*

The wait seemed endless because the outcome was open. I wasn't working, I had no money, I was still being harassed, and I had no certainty as to whether the passport would actually arrive. I would wander through the city, thin-nerved and full of the desire to scream in public. I recited poems and old bitter rhymes to myself, and invented new ones to go with them. They tamed my steps. I tried to convince myself that I would remain normal, even if I didn't get my passport and had to continue living here. I thought that maybe the city was just a map, that if I switched to the other side of the street at the right place, I might end up in West Berlin again. I played this game with myself, switching sides of the street, but I remained standing in Timişoara, in the summer heat, laughing at myself. It was like when I was a child and I thought the furniture was walking around my room at night, and I just had to flick on the light at the right time to catch it moving.

Once I had taken the decision to emigrate, I was finished with the country in my head. But my feet were still here. I couldn't read novels any more; their narrated time was at odds with my restlessness. And I was even less able to write anything that told a story. Telling a story meant staying, and I wanted to leave. I was also a bit afraid of the fact that once I had emigrated, I would no longer be here. And would never again be allowed back into the country. I was worried about my mother, who did not want to emigrate. And I was afraid of the separations I was about to endure. Most of all, I was afraid of saying goodbye to Jenny.

And once you had received the news that you were allowed to emigrate, you were still far from having a passport. You had to get hold of a docket and run from one administration to the next, gathering one stamp after another. You had to queue everywhere, waiting for hours only to be turned away and so having to line up again the next day. The stamp requirements were unhinged. You had to go all over the place, from the Office for National Cultural Heritage right through to the Office for Chimneys. I lived on the fifth floor of a ten-storey block of flats. I didn't have a chimney, but still I needed the stamp from the Chimney Office to confirm I didn't have a chimney. And you were only allowed to let two days pass between one stamp and the next. If you didn't manage to get them within this time, whatever the reason, all your stamps became invalid and you had to start all over again from the beginning. It was capricious and tyrannical, and your only defence was bribery. There was an art to correctly greasing someone's palm. Fold the bank note just the right amount, it shouldn't be too small, nor too big, then place it inside the docket in the right place, so it wouldn't slip out too early but would still be discovered in time. If the clerk didn't see it in time, you would already find yourself being yelled at and turned away. The clerks had been spoilt by the bribery and felt mistreated if someone didn't know the knack of palm-greasing.

When did you feel sure that everything would be all right? When you finally got hold of your passport, when you got on to the train, when you crossed the border?

Once we had our passports, we were sure we would be able to leave the country. We went to the Curtici border station. But while we were sitting there with our suitcases in the waiting room, we started to feel unsure again. We were waiting for the night train to Vienna, along with another ten people or so. The whole station was classified as a border zone, and no one was allowed to leave the waiting room. Three border guards walked up and down and stared into space, as if we weren't there. We sat next to each other in silence; people only spoke in hushed tones. Then everybody was subjected to a full body search. It was past midnight; you could hear the train hiss outside. One of the guards ordered us to follow him on to the platform. When we got up, another said: you three stay there.

Yes, there were three of us, my mother was there too. She was already sixty-two years old and said she was too old to emigrate. She didn't want to leave her home and her village. But then they made sure the village turned against her. That is, they showed her what would happen once I was out of the country. One morning, she was picked up at home by the village policeman and taken to the police station. The policeman ranted at her, but she didn't speak Romanian well enough to understand his threats and invectives. Once his tantrum was over, he left the room and locked the door behind him. My mother spent the whole day, right through till late in the evening, cooped up inside this room. She knocked on the door, she cried, none of it was any use. Out of desperation, and to make time pass less slowly, she started to dust the room, at first using her handkerchief. But as time continued to stand still, she picked up a towel that was hanging by the washbasin and used it to mop the floor. When she told me about this, I was appalled that she had spent the day locked up, and enraged by her self-humiliation.

After this act of bullying, she dreaded the policeman and wanted to get out of the village. And they wanted her out too. She received her forms, and then her passport, in a very short amount of time, without paying any bribes, such that she was able to emigrate with me. There was no time left for bribery and no one wanted anything anyway. I don't know whether the secret service wanted to get rid of her or if it was the village policeman. She lived in a very big house.

So now we were sitting once more, with just the three of us left in the waiting room, and we were being searched again. The policemen took their time. The station lantern shone through the window; the wind was blowing the snow diagonally through the light. Our fear that the train would leave without us kept growing.

After all the harassment that had taken place just before we left, after the staged break-in and the house search, I was no longer sure whether what we had in our hands really were passports. I once again thought anything was possible. Were they going to not let us out of the waiting room and then later say that it was our fault that we had missed the train? Were we emigrating, or were they sending us back into the country we were trying to leave? They could do whatever they wanted, after all – including pushing the game to new levels of insanity. If we weren't leaving, we would no longer have a roof over our heads. Not that it would matter anyway. You don't need a flat any more, they would say: you're going to prison.

But we *did* have passports in our hands. We were pushed out to the train at a gallop. We were still standing in the aisle as the train's engine started up. Standing on the steps up to the carriage, one of the policemen still had enough time to say: we can get you anywhere.

They also stamped a parting piece of harassment into our passports. We left the country on 28 February, but the stamp read 29 February. This day did not exist in 1987. It wasn't a leap year. And that stamp earned me untold grief from every German authority I had to deal with afterwards.

Was there a moment when you were saying goodbye
that was particularly painful, when you felt as though
something were being torn from you?

The most difficult goodbye was with Jenny. We couldn't let go of each other. She left, crying, and I closed the door. Then she knocked and I opened it again. And we cried for a while and then she left and I closed the door again.

Then she knocked again and I opened it again. And then I walked down to the street with her and watched her go for a long time. The street was dead straight and flat. It was the end of February, a frozen sun hung over the city. And it seemed to me as if the street ran downhill that day. And the further away Jenny went, the brighter her anorak shone. Or was it the tears in my eyes? Or both? I thought of a silver spoon, and that was what this moment was too. This object had nothing to do with our parting, and yet no words could better describe it.

When you arrived in Germany, in the reception centre in Nuremberg, the German secret service, who interviewed every emigrant, suspected you of being a Securitate agent and so interrogated you for days, while your mother's interview was over in a minute. Your mother was also granted German citizenship quite quickly, while you had to wait almost two years for it. How did this positively absurd reenactment of your treatment by the Romanian authorities make you feel?

I thought I was going mad, that the world had been derailed. In Romania, the Securitate suspected me of working for the BND, and now that I was in Nuremberg, the BND suspected me of working for the Securitate. You could see the grounds of Hitler's Nuremberg Rallies from the reception centre, and behind many a desk hung a map of Germany dating back to 1939.

Long before my departure, I had received letters from Germany, from so-called 'compatriots', informing me that I was not wanted in this country. This also appeared to be an organised campaign, and it fitted with the smear campaigns in the *Landsmannschaft* newspapers. These had already been running for several years, ever since *Nadirs* had been published in Romania. But the fact that in Nuremberg, in this reception centre, the BND also suspected that I was an agent – that was a shock to me. I will never forget one exchange I had with my BND interrogator:

Did you have any dealings with the Romanian secret service?

It had dealings with me, there's a difference.

Let me worry about what the difference is, that's what they pay me for after all.

I could almost hear my grandmother's voice: don't think where you shouldn't.

They presented me with folded sheets of paper with identikit faces on them; I was supposed to identify which ones were Securitate agents. I helped as much as I could. I asked my interrogator why he hadn't done any research about me before he began suspecting me. I asked why he didn't want to know how I had lived in Romania and what I thought of the dictatorship. He stuck stubbornly to his opinion; I was talking to the walls. Throughout the interrogations, right through to the final one, he would always take his leave from me unmoved, with the same sentence: if you are under orders, you could still say so now.

During the breaks between interrogations, I would go out on to the street. The afternoons got dark early. I remember the naked antlers of the trees, the snow like flour. The reception centre was called '*Langwasser*': 'Longwater'. Far too beautiful a name for a block of concrete. Diagonally across the street was Hitler's rally ground. Here and there a streetlight blazed. This place is going to swallow me up, I thought. And I was so desperate, I wouldn't have minded if it had. I would have preferred to leave Germany immediately, because I was made to feel that I wasn't wanted. But where was I supposed to go?

The only way I could explain the BND's suspicion was that they were influenced by the *Landsmannschaft*. They knew each other well, their offices were on the same corridor in the reception centre. And the *Landsmannschaft*, I thought, was influenced by the Securitate. It stunned me that the German secret service had not looked into my biography themselves, not checked what the *Landsmannschaft* was telling them. That they let themselves be 'advised' by a *Landsmannschaft* that had not ever said a critical word about the two dictatorships it was embroiled with. It was founded by former Nazi officials after the Second World War and its leadership at the time included diligent bureaucrats who had emigrated from the Ceaușescu dictatorship. The overlap between these two dictatorships could also be seen in the language used in the smear pieces published in the *Landsmannschaft* newspapers. I was accused of 'pathological rejection' and 'hatred' towards 'my Swabian tribe'. I was apparently one of 'the most valuable employees of the Bucharest Central Committee Propaganda Department' and was damaging 'the image of German expatriates in their motherland'. I was called an 'asphalt literature writer', the term which Goebbels used to bad-mouth authors who did not 'emerge from' German 'folklore'. Another article in one of those newspapers ended with the quote 'to each his own': the inscription on the gate of the Buchenwald concentration camp.

We were also given a docket in the reception centre, much the same as the one we had before leaving Romania.

We needed a stamp from the *Landsmannschaft*. I had to go into their office as a supplicant and was received with glee. You could tell just by looking at me, the clerk said to me, that the German air was not doing me any good.

The BND had no interest at all in what you could tell them about the dictatorship?

The only thing that was political about the interrogations was the BND's suspicion that I was an agent – they weren't interested at all in the reality of the dictatorship. The BND didn't want to know anything about my life, or they wouldn't have been able to keep this suspicion alive. This strategy reminded me of the Securitate's tactic of only presenting me with fabrications, so that we avoided discussing reality. How is this possible, I asked myself? Despite there being no contact between them, both secret services were following the same script. I wasn't physically afraid of the BND, but I felt profoundly depressed by them. Whatever I said, with both the Securitate and the BND, I couldn't change anything about this fabricated suspicion that was directed at me – and this realisation was cataclysmic.

The authorities kept trying to get me to tick the 'family reunion' box as the reason for my emigration. I was told that I had to decide whether I was German or politically persecuted. And I said: both.

Both, they said, is not an option, we don't have a form for that.

My Friend Oskar

Earlier on, you described writing as a combination of fascination and tedium. On top of this comes the fact that the past, when it resurfaces in the present, becomes painfully alive. The fears, the capricious tyranny you were at the mercy of, the pain over your dead friends, the rage over your stolen existence — none of it is ever truly over.

Yes, there is an urgency to writing, it is a necessity, but one that immediately comes up against internal resistance. I always write for and against myself. I never write anything down until it is unavoidable. I put it off because I know that, once I get started, it will take possession of me and I will be afraid of it. Writing swallows me whole. Language abolishes time; it pulls your experience into an obsessive search for word, rhythm and sound. This precision has a ruthlessness to it, but also has an undertow that I can no longer find my way out of. I am wrapped up in it. I think that this preserves me, too. Writing has a magnetism to it, otherwise I would not have been doing it for years. I believe that this magnetism comes from the interplay between the ruthlessness of the act and the fact that writing is also a means of self-preservation. Perhaps I frame it as 'ruthless-ness' because I didn't choose my subjects myself, because my writing is full of stolen life and the tyranny of other people. And perhaps I talk of 'preservation' because I fear that I would have been utterly defenceless against what I have experienced had these words – which were so hard to find – not come to my aid. Out of writing emerges a kind of word hunger. New words are formed which show me something that I would not have seen without them.

My experience stares me in the face once more when I write, but with a different gaze, glassy and unnatural. As if on the one hand this experience knows itself perfectly, and on the other not at all. What has happened happens again when you are writing. This is why nothing you have experienced is ever finished – and whether an experience goes well or goes awry depends entirely on the language you find to describe it. Out of this discord comes procras-tination and my fear that I am no match for this glassy, unnatural gaze. But even if I procrastinate, I always end up starting to write at some point. I think I have been relying on my writing for years. Over time, this has led to an outward habit of attempting to look at my life afresh through language. But then this also means enduring it again. And the habit always contains the fear that I won't manage to both look at my life and endure it again. This double doubt is part of it, though. Otherwise, you have already lost.

Are there drafts that you have thrown out?

Perhaps not thrown out, but I've definitely temporar-ily given up on drafts before. I've then tackled them again later. The beginning of anything is almost always unusable. I'm also often fed up with first-person narrators. But then when I see, in the second, third or fourth chapter, that the sentence acquires a different sensuality when there is an 'I' in there, then I have to accept that the text is insisting on the first person, even if I may well be tired of it. And when a manuscript seems to be finished, I read over it again twenty times. Every reading conjures up a new version. These are often detours, and I end up coming back to the very first version, but it is not for nothing: I only know that the very first version is the valid one once I have tried out twenty other possibilities.

It's exactly the same when I read one of my earlier texts. I wouldn't change anything about the content, just the breath of the sentences.

What do you start with when you begin a new book?
The span of time you want to write about, particular
situations, which people will feature? What is the
germ of an idea that you begin each book with?

The starting point is often just a single situation, but a situation which, as it then emerges in the writing, turns out to more or less know the whole story already. 'More or less' is the opposite of precisely, however, and when you are writing things must be precise. 'More or less' means that you still have to labour to find the meshwork, the structure, the order of the story. Writing then becomes about what to mention and what to omit, about hinting and insisting, drawing out and paring down, exciting and quenching, clarifying and withholding – and all of this simultaneously. You can feel how the weights shift, how the logic of reality submits to language. You can't tell stories any other way. I cannot foretell, nor even foresee, how language will dismantle my understanding of what I have experienced, how it will take it apart and put it back together again differently, until it is captured, to some degree, in a particular order of words. A sequence of words becomes an invented truth. Everything is artificially constructed, but the unreal is made valid in the text through my use of the right language. The language must be beautiful precisely because the topic is threatening. I wouldn't be able to bear writing if it were not for the invented truth of language, in which what is beautiful is painful.

All of my works were born out of such starting points. One exception is *The Hunger Angel*. For this book is not about my own life, but about my mother's deportation. Even as a child, I could sense that my mother's back was bent under a heavy burden. I would often hear the village word for deportation – '*Verschleppung*', 'abduction' – but as a child I didn't understand what it meant. As a child I was always under the impression that my mother was very old, but in fact she was barely thirty. And I found eating alone with her uncanny. I was infected by her anxiety and greed as we ate, it was as though we were desperately chasing satiety. In the process, your mouth was working entirely by itself; it did not belong to anything or anybody. This grim way of eating made you feel very lonely.

Potatoes were the staple food in the camp, and for my mother they have remained sacred to this day. I had to learn how to peel potatoes. My mother demanded that the peel be in one piece: wafer-thin and circular, like a coiled ribbon. She would scream at me if my knife slipped too deep into the potato or if I had to shift the turn of the knife and tore the ribbon. She gave me a beating if the potato slices were irregular or crooked when I cut them. Her chronic hunger, once she had returned from the camp, was the source of her lifelong complicity with the potato and of my distance from the potato. As if it were the potato itself setting these exacting requirements that were almost impossible to meet and calling for this stringent form of respect. If every person has an object outside themselves that instructs them on how they are supposed to shape their lives, then for my mother it is unquestionably the potato.

You were born just three years after your mother's
return; her deportation still weighed heavily on her.
As a child, you could sense the horror, but you had
no concept of where it came from.

I didn't understand the word 'abduction' and I didn't understand the word 'camp'. And because the State prohibited people from talking about the deportations, these words were never really said out loud – they were only ever secrets and whispers. And so these words, because of the way they existed between us, became all the more charged. The silences, the avoidance and the tight-lipped insinuations blew these words out of proportion for me as a child; they became another of the forbidden things you would constantly be dwelling on in your head. I was almost afraid of these words. My mother would often mention how people's heads were shaved in the camp as she combed my hair. And that didn't just enter my head, but my whole body; it made my flesh creep. I don't know if this is what she wanted. I didn't understand anything about deportation, but still I suffered from it.

'Deportation' was the sum of all the scattered monstrosities that loomed over my childhood and can be found in my writing as early as my first book, *Nadirs*, in the form of hunger and grass soup and freezing and shaven heads. And I already thought at the time that it wasn't enough to address it in a marginal storyline; someone needed to write a whole book about deportation. I thought this for twenty-five years, but I would always shy away from it and write a different book instead. For in my head the subject of deportation never stopped being loaded with menace.

Your conversations with Oskar Pastior about his time in the labour camp became central to The Hunger Angel. *Were they also the catalyst for you finally daring to tackle this subject?*

No, I had researched it for years. My mother would keep telling me who of her acquaintances from the village had died. And they were always deportees. Time is running away from me, I told myself: soon they will all be dead and no one will be able to tell us anything any more. In order to write a book, I felt that I needed a lot of people to tell me about their experiences. I tried to make up for lost time by meeting deportees. But these were people who were not used to talking about themselves, and so the conversations all went the same way. They remained stuck in generalities. They included neither the daily life of the camp nor what was personal about this great tragedy. Any details that would have described the camp more tangibly were buried inside them. And the same went for published testimonies: I of course found many complaints about the suffering, but it was always framed as a collective experience. There was only this 'we'. But I needed the experiences of individuals in order to tell the story of this collective experience.

Then, I got lucky. I was travelling with Oskar Pastior to a reading in South Tyrol. We were passing through the mountains, and I said that fir trees are lazy. I said that they do nothing, that they never change, and instead always remain the same shade of green. Deciduous trees have buds, flowers, fruit, they take on a host of colours, throw off their leaves – they work hard. I said I didn't understand why, out of all the trees, we put fir trees up in our living rooms at Christmas, with tinsel hanging off them like entrails. And Oskar Pastior became angry. He started to defend fir trees. In the camp, he said, the fir trees were your last contact with civilisation. He told me about this fir tree he had made out of his green woollen gloves, which he had unravelled – how he knotted the wool on to a wire frame, how the thick threads looked like fir needles. He told me how this Christmas tree – no bigger than his hand – brought joy to the barracks. And then, at the end, Pastior added: you don't have to believe in Christmas to believe in the fir tree. Well, that made me gulp. It also made me reflect on the fact that he was a mountain person, while I was from the plain. He didn't just like the mountains and the fir trees and the forest, he accepted them as his home. While I rejected my home – the plain and the cornfield and the river valley – Pastior was constantly tailoring his home to fit him, like a shirt that is never finished, so that it would stay with him. He liked his forest of fir trees, he liked his mountain ranges, whereas I have always spurned my cornfield and my river valley.

Pastior ostensibly met the outside world with acceptance – but his internal response is visible in the way his poetry plays with broken language. That is what was so magnificent about him. He also liked the smallest, most kitsch porcelain figurines from back home. He was, after all – and this is what was so crazy – extremely conventional. He was a conventional person with the craziest ideas. I found it so beautiful. He was also the most narcissistic person while also remaining the most modest. He contained these opposites, which ordinarily never come together – that was what I thought was so wonderful about him.

With his defence of the fir trees, Pastior told me, quite by-the-by, exactly what I had always tried to find out about the camp.

I knew that if I were to talk to Pastior for just a quarter of an hour, I would find out more than if I had spoken to other people for months. But I didn't tell him that. Nor did I dare ask him whether he could tell me more. After his defence of the fir trees, I knew that all of his memories would be this sharp. I thought that talking about the horrors of the camp with this precision must be painful, and I did not want to impose this on him. I was worried about him. My admiration for his books also made me shy. How often had I read in secret from the copy of *The Crimean Gothic Fan** I kept in my half-open drawer in the machine factory in Romania? The crazy courtyards he describes in this book – 'the Paraputes courtyard, the courtyard of the wind-oldest' – were not surreal in the slightest when considered next to the dendritic grounds of

---

* *Der krimgotische Fächer: Lieder und Balladen* [The Crimean Gothic Fan: Songs and Ballads] was a book of what might roughly be called nonsense poetry by Pastior; it was published in Germany in 1978.

the factory. It was as if Pastior had been to this factory long before me – the courtyards from his book were so real. *The Crimean Gothic Fan*, with its enchanted images, seemed to understand better than I did just how dangerous the environment I was living in was. I also created a kind of magic formula for myself based on parts of sentences from Pastior's verses: 'Mint mint flaumiram schpectrum.' When I could no longer endure life, I would comfort myself with this dictum. That which scores of literary critics viewed as meaningless linguistic acrobatics is still to this day, for me, the description of a world derailed. With 'flaumiram schpectrum' I was, half-jokingly but also sadly, asking the mint for some perspective. The mint, specifically, because in Romanian to rub mint means to waste time.

I told the story of Pastior's defence of the fir trees to Ernest Wichner,* who was much closer to him and was overseeing the publication of his works. He knew that I had been struggling with my research into the camps for quite some time already. And he asked Oskar Pastior whether he would talk to me about his five years in the camps for a book. Oskar Pastior did not just immediately accept, he wanted to start right away. And three days later, I went to visit him for the first time.

How did you structure your conversations?

Our meetings always began in the same way: I would arrive on Mondays at three o'clock. But the length of time

------

*   Ernest Wichner (born 1952) is a German writer of Banat Swabian origin, and was one of the founding members of the *Aktions-gruppe Banat*.

I stayed with him kept growing the more we spoke, the more I wrote. It became normal for me to stay until gone midnight, sometimes later. And even then I had to slow Pastior down, because he wouldn't get tired. There was an urgency to his accounts, I realised, for this was the very first time that he was talking about the camp after thirty years of silence.

I wanted to use my voice recorder again, but Pastior refused to speak into it. It was too impersonal for him, and it intimidated him. So I bought big notebooks to write things down in. My note-taking didn't bother him. And on paper he could also draw objects from the camp for me: the coal shovels, the clogs, the clothes, the cooling tower, the cattle cars. These drawings came naturally, and I am glad that they exist, along with my notes. A voice recorder would have required an entirely different rhythm and an entirely different methodology. Whether he had already considered this, I don't know, but, even if it was just an instinctive resistance to the device, he was right. With a recorder you have to fast-forward, rewind; you can't correct anything, you can only record it again. Afterwards, you may no longer know your way around it yourself. And we would have had nothing physical, nothing in black and white, to refer to while we were sitting there together. The written word gave us something to hold on to.

Which details were you particularly interested in, what did you ask about?

Above all, I was interested in the seemingly unimportant, the inconspicuous. I wanted a personal description of the camp, from an individual, to capture its so-called 'everyday life'. So I asked very simple questions, at first about external, concrete details about the camp. What did the clothes look like? What about the dishes? The dormitory, the barracks, the grounds, the cooling tower? A host of details, which together made up the world of the camp. And after that came ever more questions about what was going on inside the forced labourers. How did you know what time it was? Did you have a mirror? How long does one remain vain? Are vanity and dignity the same thing? What does chronic hunger mean? How does one perceive oneself when undernourished and dystrophic? There were no quick, easy answers to these questions. And Pastior, as he spoke to me, was thinking about them for the first time, for in the camp he did not constantly see himself from the outside. He wouldn't have been able to bear it.

He would keep saying how he had been dreaming about the camp for sixty years, but that his dreams now revolved around being deported from Berlin to various places. Just as with my mother, the camp remained hidden inside him: in certain habits – in the smallest habits – that was what was so terrible about it. It was there in the way he ate, which was entirely different to the way my mother did, but similarly unnatural. With my mother, it was as if she was running away from the food that she was eating, greedily. With Pastior, it was as if he was disappearing entirely into the food. He ate slowly, with his whole body, with all the pores of his skin. He ate heartily, almost desperately – but happily. He was also absent, though, like my mother. You were excluded; you had no business with his hunger.

Pastior answered my questions precisely. Sometimes, if I came back to him on something, he would correct me. And then I knew that he had spent the whole week thinking about my question. My mother can't even tell me whether there were fifteen people in her barracks or sixty. Perhaps she herself no longer knew this even shortly after her return, perhaps she had blocked it out because she couldn't bear it. Or she knows it to this day but cannot bring herself to say. I had to ask myself whether recollection has more to do with a person's memory or with their disposition. Or whether it is solely how one perceives an experience at the time that determines what one will remember and what one will forget later on. Pastior's memory impressed me, because his gaze had registered every little thing. Everything that Pastior told me about, and how he told me about it, was as if it were by-the-by. But for me it was essential.

Did this process also lead to some memories coming back to him or perhaps becoming clearer?

Definitely. He demonstrated work processes for me: how he unloaded coal using the heart-shovel, his favourite shovel. Or how he carried cinder blocks in the dark, from the cement mixer to the press and further along to the drying area. It was like theatre. At first it was funny, because he would stand up and swing his arms; he would lift and dip his air shovel. He would change the position of his legs, of his heels, of his toes and of the soles of his feet, depending on whether he was unloading from the front edge of the wagon or the middle, or the remnants of the coal right at the back. He spoke of different ways of saving your strength, of the fencing stance, and of the graceful dance of working with a shovel, the movements as smooth as gliding across the ice on skates. But these scenes were sad too, because every movement was inscribed on his body. I had to watch how Oskar Pastior was being pulled back into the camp again and meeting his past self. Standing there, on the carpet in his room, he was in two places at once: he returned to the camp in his head while pantomiming the action before my eyes. And I noticed that he was amazed at himself, perhaps even shocked. He was demonstrating these actions for the first time sixty years later; he surely had no idea that his body had preserved its own memories, which his head knew nothing of.

Our conversations were always unpredictable. We would stumble upon new details, and I would ask questions that I would otherwise not have been able to ask.

He told me about the different kinds of sand he got to know in the camp, and which coal was his favourite. He viewed every material he had to work with – cement, sand, coal, cinder, stones – as good or evil, and he ascribed intentionality to all materials: they were either sympathetic or hostile. And not just the material, the snow too, the wind, and the orach, which grew bitter as it reddened and became bedecked with flowers – at which point you couldn't eat it any more. It rejected you when it was at its most beautiful. The most complicated relationship he had was to hunger, which could be a violent, tender, shy or frivolous hunger angel. Personifying this relationship was Pastior's way of trying to protect his dignity from humiliation through hunger.

Such a precise sense of perception can be dangerous. But, on the other hand, it can also save you, for you can cling on to it. It is a substitute for the privacy which has been taken from you; it is a remnant of your own will, enduring within the system of a camp that is otherwise ruled only by despotism.

*Humiliation through hunger – this means one is
pushed into situations, or forced to take actions
in which one becomes foreign to oneself?*

In a place where people die of starvation every day, your relationship to food is reduced to greed and ruthlessness. An emaciated, half-starved person can't think past their hunger, because it tortures them every second. Even your sleep is infiltrated with hunger, your dreams exclusively circle around food.

Hunger extinguishes all civilising standards, and thus makes its own laws – and they are brutal. Hunger makes you brutal.

Over the course of my research, I read books about the camps of the gulag. It is astounding: in all types of Russian camps, whether under military or civilian leadership, the same hierarchies and patterns of behaviour developed among the inmates. The bread court from Pastior's labour camp existed in all other camps too. By 'bread court', I mean the process by which bread thieves were punished by death: they were beaten to death by common consent. And the death sentence for the thief justified itself: because the missing bread would also be a death sentence for some-one else; because the thief wanted to save themselves at the expense of the person they had stolen from, leaving them to starve to death. The violence of the bread court cannot be compared to hungerless violence. Really, hunger is the greatest violence, it robs all other feelings of their validity and effect. And even when these feelings persist, they have no chance against hunger, against this wild physical craving for survival, this naked egomania. There were cases in the camp where a person would take their spouse's food from the canteen each day, leaving them to starve to death. They did so with their eyes wide open, despite their love for this person – or rather, it was precisely their love that gave them the right to do this.

What is a marriage compared to a hunger that has already devoured over half of you? In the camp, nobody knew how to share, love, or be married any more; they certainly didn't know how to be hungry. Love may have endured, but it was of no use to them there. Pastior spoke of it as the time of skin and bones.

At the start, you were simply taking notes about what Oskar Pastior was telling you, but at some point the idea emerged of working together on a book. How did this come about?

Taking notes was the first step, and it lasted for over a year. Every time, I would read aloud the notes I had taken before going home. And when I came back again a week later, my notes from the previous session were read aloud again. Only then would we move on to another question. But often new details would have occurred to Pastior: tiny things that would then lead me to entirely different questions and him to an entirely different way of approaching the topic. We would get stuck on these changes all day, until I had to go back home. Sometimes we would talk about the same thing two, three times.

I had a list of questions on the final pages of my notebook. All the answers would result in more questions, since the more I found out, the more questions I had. If a new question occurred to me, I would immediately add it to the list. Then, once the majority of the questions from my list had been dealt with, I would read all the notes I had made once more. And then, bit by bit, we would grapple with the pulse of Pastior's oral narration and rephrase it. It was this oral narration that gave us the titles of the first few chapters. They mirror his relationship to daily life in the camp: 'On coal', 'Cinder blocks', 'Fir trees', 'On the hunger angel'. This repetition in his way of phrasing things gave our first revision of the notes a structure which allowed for a connection to be created between my external gaze and his internal gaze. For in those sessions, Pastior always had to get out of the camp, and I had to get into it. There were two different orientations meeting in our sessions. What memories from inside the camp were needed? What did Pastior need? And what would a literary text need later on, on top of his account? We didn't know back then how far it could remain factual and how far it would have to become fiction. As far as Pastior was concerned, it was biographical, and therefore factual, but his reality was full of poetry.

Then, when I was working at home, I would select individual chapters and expand the notes I had taken with fictitious material. I would write individual scenes and read them out to Oskar Pastior at our next meeting. At first he felt betrayed by them: a first-person narrator was now doing whatever they wanted with his recollections. Pastior initially bridled at the fact that the first-person narrator is involved in the bread court's violent brawl. I understood how difficult it was for him to move from the painful proximity of lived experience to the distance inherent to a work of fiction. I had to give Oskar Pastior time to grow to like this first-person narrator. I wanted him to like him, but not mistake himself for him. However similar they may be, he should know that they were not one and the same.

Sometimes I would come to him and say: I've changed something in a chapter again. And it would look as if all we had to discuss was the single sentence I'd tweaked, but then we would spend the whole day, from three o'clock to midnight, working on that one problem and I would take yet more notes. The next day, Pastior would type up the edited text on his mechanical typewriter. And he would despair when I came along the week after that and said: we have to change one more thing. But I've just typed it up and now you want to change it again, he would say in a grim and bitter tone, before adding: I never knew prose was so difficult. And then we would laugh.

Despite being such close friends, as authors you are very different. Did you quickly agree on the fundamentals of the text?

We didn't agree, but we never quarrelled. I would often already be rephrasing things as I was taking notes. Pastior himself knew when his memories were becoming sentimental or 'overly cloying', as he would say. I allowed Oskar Pastior his sentimentality, he had to be kind towards himself to survive in the camp. And once he had returned home, he had to be kind towards himself in order to live with the memory for all those years. Sometimes I would say: that's not good for the text. Or: do you want to make yourself look better than the others? He didn't, of course.

Only with time did I learn that the effects of deportation are insidious — as cruel and intimate as hunger itself. Aside from the body's torment, the damage also takes the shape of an addiction. One dreads the camp, while developing a homesickness for it. And it consumes the survivor.

It continues to humiliate him long after he has escaped, because it enchants him against his will. This insight inspired the phrase about the hunger angel 'deceiving me with my own flesh' in the novel.

In the middle of this work, Oskar Pastior died very unexpectedly. You had to finish the project alone. What consequences did this rupture have for you, for the book?

The main difficulty was the balance between dread of the camp and homesickness for it. Sentimentality is normal when you are remembering something. But the text could not veer into longing for the camp. Nor, however, could it deny this feeling – it should reflect it. After Oskar Pastior's death, I had to negotiate this balancing act with myself. I wouldn't have been able to at all earlier on.

When we disagreed, Pastior would often say: I'm giving it to you. And by 'it', he meant the whole awful topic. Ah, you think it's that simple? I would say. You say I'm giving it to you, but you're not getting out of it that easily . . .

Yes. But then he did get out of it after all – he went away, he went and died. This sudden death was a shock. And it remained unreal. He died in Frankfurt, so I didn't see his body. There was an urn, and we buried that, not him. I missed him so much. And in the turmoil of my grief, it seemed as if he had managed to evade the whole awful topic after all. I bargained for his return in my thoughts and promised him that he would not need to have anything more to do with the text if he did. I also scolded him for leaving me alone with all my notes. I reproached him for it and saw his face as I did so.

I couldn't touch the notes again for a whole year; just looking at my notebooks was painful. Each session would have a date against it. He was particularly fastidious about always recording the date; it was a superstition he had. And when something couldn't be explained in words he turned to the drawings. And in every sentence that I now read, I could hear his voice. It was sometimes euphoric, sometimes heavy and low.

In my grief, I kept returning to the thought that our years of work could not be for nothing. After all, I had long resolved to write about my mother's deportation, because the word 'abduction' had loomed over my childhood. So too had Oskar Pastior's abduction loomed over his whole life, and precisely because of this I owed it to him, I thought, to attempt to tell this story. Besides, he had always said I should do it on my own. When his despondency got the upper hand, he would even say he wasn't sure he believed himself; he even questioned whether he really had been in the camp. And then I would say: you don't need to prove anything; everyone believes it, apart from you. He would smile grimly and say: but that doesn't help me at all. And now he had bequeathed the whole awful topic to me in such a way that, in spite of my grief, I couldn't reject it.

When I started to write the book in earnest, I wanted to change as little as possible. But it didn't work: I noticed that I couldn't be two people, I couldn't be Oskar Pastior as well as myself. I had to detach myself from the initial structure of the text, take my leave of the 'we' and give myself permission to use 'I', to write it *my* way, not *our* way. Just as Pastior had invented names for all the real people he wrote about, I needed an invented name for the first-person narrator. I was annoyed because I had neglected to ask him what he would like his alter ego to be called in the book. I gave him the name Leo Auberg. The book as we had imagined it was supposed to be a poetic documentation of the camp.

But then, once I was alone with my notebooks and had read through them again, it became clear to me that without Pastior I could only write a novel, and that Leo Auberg would have to be its protagonist. Because the notes were merely a phenomenology of the camp. Tools, clothes, watchtowers, barracks, the factory, the coke ovens and the cooling tower, the dishes – it was all described in detail and had even been sketched by Pastior. It formed a strong bedrock of lifeless things. But there was no camp life in my notes – I knew far too little about the people and their stories. So instead I would build my novel on the bedrock of my notes.

At first, I used marginal notes as launching points. For example, a remark of Pastior's about once having found ten roubles became the chapter about the market. Or I'd expand on the story of Kati Sentry, who was mentally disabled and didn't even know where she was. What was her day-to-day life like? What did she do and what did she say? How did she survive? I had to invent all of this. She was a handful of sentences in my notes, little more than a name. But she needed to become a person. So I imagined myself into her, such that she became one of my favourite characters in the novel.

And of course, Leo Auberg also needed a family, he needed memories. We had been so immersed in the camp that Pastior's return and the time after that had not come up, even though without this return there would have been no one to speak about the camp. The starting point for *The*

Hunger Angel is that of an old architect looking back. In hindsight, the fact that we did not broach these topics is also astonishing because Pastior talked so much about his homesickness.

> *At some point in the novel, we realise there is nothing for Leo Auberg outside the camp. In one scene you describe how, after having been sent away from the camp for the day, to a farm to harvest potatoes, he returns late at night, and calls the way back the 'way home'. The camp has become everything to him.*

All I knew based on my notes was that Oskar Pastior had been sent to a kolkhoz some distance away, and was given the chance while he was there to eat some of the potatoes he had been harvesting. He ate so many that he could barely walk home afterwards; he had to go slowly, and did not arrive at the camp until late in the evening.

We never discussed what this felt like. That I then had to invent. What was it like to be making his way 'home' alone through the night? What thoughts were whirring through his head? Was he wondering if it might be possible to escape? And if so, where would he go? In the flat steppe, all those who had tried to leave had been caught and brought back to the camp half-dead. And then they would disappear forever.

Yes, at some point the deportees had been so hollowed out that, to them, nothing existed outside the camp. All that was left was to come to terms with the camp, resigning yourself to the drills and the neglect so that you didn't lose your mind, or resort to killing yourself out of despair. One year bled into the next, until five years had gone by.

And during this miserably long time, the internees were never told whether they would ever be allowed home. Part of their punishment, as well as the forced labour and the hunger, was this uncertainty over how long they would remain in the camp. It was interminable, and so the homesickness became a disease. Their chronic longing for home was like their chronic hunger, always there. It was a homesickness that, with time, lost its connection to the place they had come from and instead took shape against the steppe – and, in so doing, became even greater and more obsessive.

I imagined how Pastior must have felt, steeped in this general, smouldering homesickness, on his way back from the potato field to the camp. He was walking all alone through the vastness of the steppe. It was no place for people to be at night; it certainly wasn't any kind of place to live. In the camp however were his barracks, and in the barracks his bed and under his pillow the bread he had saved – so this was his home. There was nothing else for it but to call his way back to the camp the way home. Pastior often told me that he did not feel homesick, that instead he suffered from a lack of homesickness. It seemed to me that he was on his guard against the word 'homesick'. He had warded off the word, so that the feeling would not devour him. For nobody could save themselves from this feeling. Like all the others interned there, he had been constantly thinking about home. Above all, about his grandmother saying: I know you'll come back. But this sentence is pure homesickness and the sentence, as he himself put it, saved him. And so homesickness also saved him. The smouldering, general homesickness, which he would only accept as a lack of homesickness.

*The homesickness and the hunger angel came with
him when he left the camp – even once he was home
they wouldn't leave him. At one point you write:
'my family, I'll say, and I will mean the people
from the camp.'*

After he returns home, Leo Auberg is no longer recog-
nisable, either to himself or to his family. He is a change-
ling, and he cannot arrive at the place that one calls home,
precisely because this place has remained the same. He is
now in a foreign land, but one that he knows through and
through, and in his head is born a homesickness for the
camp – despite the horror that almost killed him there. He
remains feral inside, incapable of relationships; he can no
longer relax his grip on himself. In the novel, I also write: 'I
won't ever let anyone cling to me again, I [. . .] am unreach-
able out of humility, not pride.'

*Oskar Pastior's sudden death made your trip to
Ukraine together even more significant. It provided
you with a foundation for additions and inventions.*

Oskar Pastior's vocabulary of landscape was rooted in
the mountains. He described the steppe to me as a mountainous landscape, he talked of ravines and scarped terrain.
But on our trip I saw only plains; the small areas of raised
ground in the middle were slag heaps. And his relationship
to plants was a relationship to plant names. He liked the
word lavender, and so he talked about lavender, but what
he then showed me in the steppe was bird vetch: a plant
with indigo-blue flowers and thin tendrils which cling to
other plants. I was only able to understand and describe the

way home from the market or the way to the kolkhoz or the way back to the camp from the potato field because I had made this journey to the steppe. I had seen its infinite vastness, and the light at different times of day and the colours of the sky. I didn't know beforehand how much I would be dependent on my impressions from this trip, how important the journey would turn out to be.

I paid careful attention to the grasses, bushes and trees in the steppe and in the villages – to the orach, the thistles and the wild dill – because I have an intimate connection to plants. I was alone so often as a child in the whistling green valley with the cows. And in the flat steppe of Ukraine, I encountered the plants of Banat once more. Plants define a place for me, even to this day. What grows in a place is not irrelevant. Just like it is not irrelevant whether someone comes from a mountainous region or from the plains or if they grew up by the sea. The landscape is the first thing that challenges us existentially – unconsciously, too – as early as childhood. It is against this landscape that we question who we are. We offer up the transient matter of our bodies to the permanence of a landscape. Even if plants vanish in the winter, they return in the spring. While we simply disappear under the earth.

The more concrete details Pastior told me about, the less he believed he really had been in the camp. He desperately wanted to go to Ukraine and show me the steppe.

What do you think he was expecting to get from this journey? How did he feel when he returned there?

I think he wanted to show himself the camp, rather than show it to me. And I think he wanted to prove to the camp that he had not just survived, but that he was still alive. We only understood this when we got there. Ernest Wichner had gone with us: we were afraid that Pastior might break down. We bought flexible plane tickets especially, so that we would be able to fly back at any time. But things turned out very differently; Pastior couldn't tear himself away.

We visited both camps he had been interned in. There was nothing remaining of the first. And while the second camp was in ruins, everything that Pastior had described to me – buildings, equipment – remained standing or lying on the abandoned factory site as if frozen in time. Only the barracks were gone, because a law from the 1950s in the Soviet Union had mandated the destruction of what remained of the camps, even the graveyards. But the site was just as desolate as back then, when the forced labourers had arrived there to repair the war damage, such that he immediately felt at home again. He identified with everything; he would say 'our cooling tower'. He was in mourning, because after years spent rebuilding it, Socialism had destroyed his factory. It can't have all been in vain, he said.

He didn't get tired all day, he just walked around, positioning himself at the window where the food was handed out and taking an imaginary tin bowl in his hands, or showing us how he moved between the pipes, telling us the smells associated with different areas, or where and how he had lain down on the ground when he had his first moment of peace, or where he had to plant the black poplar saplings in the winter. These poplars showed just how much time had passed, because they now loomed above us, tall and strong.

Even the 'zeppelin', a monstrous, gigantic rusted pipe that was used as a 'by-the-hour hotel' for trysts between the women from the camp and the German POWs, still lay in the high grass, and the skeletons of the coke ovens stood in a row. The stairs that Oskar Pastior had used to go down to the cellar were still there. He showed us where the coal would arrive, the rails and the yama – the giant pit into which the coal was unloaded. It was as if Oskar Pastior was drunk. On the first evening, he said to me: now I have fed my soul. He was happy. I'd never heard such an expression from him before; this wasn't his usual language at all. It was unheard of, a tragic happiness.

On our first evening there, I was the one who fell apart. I went up to my bedroom, shut the door, and once I started to cry, I couldn't stop. I couldn't bear it, nor could I bear the double-edged sword of Oskar's happiness. We had spent the whole day driving through miserable places, and seen these old men who had no shoes and no teeth, but whose chests were covered in decorations from the Second World War, proudly worn on torn-up clothes. We were so foreign here and they were so friendly.

It was also important to me to see what a Ukrainian market looked like, and during our visit there Pastior bought himself a bag of chocolate biscuits, which were hard as plaster inside. Being diabetic, he wasn't supposed to eat them, but he immediately devoured the whole bag. He wouldn't have done this in Berlin, but in Ukraine he would hurry to eat. He had already eaten an unusually large amount for breakfast in the morning. Oskar, you're eating such endless amounts, I eventually said, I'm finding it unsettling. His response unsettled me even more: I have to pay my respects to this food. This too is a sentence that he would never have said anywhere else. It was the place that said this; it came from his other, past life.

Long after Pastior's death, I saw Harald Jung's portrait of Jorge Semprún: '*Mein Leben/Ma vie*' [*My Life*]. In the film, the old man Jorge Semprún visits Buchenwald concentration camp, where he was as a young man. And during his visit, he walks across the site and is so relieved that Jung is surprised by him. Semprún says simply that he has come home. It was the same with Oskar Pastior. It was trauma. Something that buries itself so deep inside your body that it destroys and enchants you. I understood then that damage is an intimate connection.

Drawers and Letters

Your office is full of cut-out words, printed in all colours, lying on all available horizontal surfaces, even on the sofa, the footstool, the window ledge. Brochures, magazines, catalogues are strewn all over the floor – they are raw materials for your collages. This is reminiscent of the little girl in Nitzkydorf, who sat in the wooden barrel with the multicoloured scraps of fabric in her aunt's tailoring workshop and sewed them into clothes for her dolls and cats.

My beautiful aunt with her porcelain skin and copper-red hair and freckles – how I loved her. But there is an important difference. She did not have a separate seamstress's shop; her workshop was her flat, and in the evening they would eat at the table she worked at during the day. She had to tidy everything up every day. I was allowed to crawl through the room with a magnet and the pins would jump up from the floor on to it. Then we would sweep up and the scraps of fabric would be put into a big wooden barrel. I learnt a lot from my aunt: cross-stitching, hemming, sewing buttonholes, invisible mending. I couldn't draw, but I had clever hands for sewing.

I can't tidy up my words any more. I do have another small room with filing cabinets for them, and I will often put them away, but not often enough, not as quickly as new ones are added to them. I keep cutting out new words. Sometimes they make me feel so weary, because they're all around me and I can no longer bear the sight of them. I feel full of them, and I am fed up with them. And when this happens, I sweep them together and simply put them in the bin. When I do this, I am throwing away hours and hours of work.

Just like my aunt, I didn't have my own workshop at first. I started my collages at the kitchen table. I had to move the words on to a chopping board in the evening so that we would be able to eat.

*Weren't the collages born as greeting cards you would
send to your friends when you were travelling?*

That's how it started. When I was on a trip, I would look for black and white postcards suited to the friends I was sending them to, or that suited me, as the person who was writing them. I rarely found such postcards. Only ever the same crude, ugly blue sky, the same kitschy view of a place. So instead, one day I bought myself index cards and I started cutting out photos from magazines on the train or plane – this was when you were still allowed to take nail scissors with you – and I would fool around, sticking a few words on there to go with them: 'the pickpocket is me' or 'insofar and first of all'. It was little more than a silly game, but it showed me how much individual words have to offer. It fascinated me, and I started to stick words on to cards at home too. There were words waiting everywhere, all I needed to do was cut them out. They existed outside me, and so I didn't have to search for them inside my head like I did when I was writing.

How do you decide which words to cut out?

I don't – it's intuitive. For every word that I cut out, I assume that I will need it at some point, otherwise I wouldn't be cutting it out. But what determines that – I don't know. There are also words that I like, of course. For example the word 'carousel', which, however often I own it, I will always cut out whenever it bumps into me. This has to do with the object, with the swing carousel on the marketplace in my village, which played music. The seats would fly almost horizontally at the end of their chains and the tips of your feet were right up in the sky; the sky flew with you. When you reached the end of a turn the music would stop, and you could hear the engine clatter and it smoked a little and it smelt of axle grease, nicely bitter. I liked riding on carousels as a child. I wouldn't buy myself sweets, but I would fritter all my money away on the carousel. The people who ran it would camp next to the village pond, and their foreignness was appealing. When I cut out the word, I am carving out everything I experienced on the carousel.

There are some words that I cannot bear because of what I have lived through, and so I do not cut them out. 'Powerful' for example. This is specific to me. Take M. Blecher,*

---

* M. Blecher (1909–38) was a Romanian writer whose texts were heavily inspired by the Modernists and Surrealists. He died aged twenty-eight of tuberculosis, leaving behind a small but influential corpus of work.

for example: in *Adventures in Immediate Unreality*, the word 'powerful' appears very often. But Blecher is such a great author and knows so well how to use this word that, without saying it, its opposite is reflected within it. With Blecher, it feels as if 'fragility' needs the word 'powerful'. Similarly, with him diminutives aren't there to make things smaller – instead they are threatening, they make things darker.

When I cut words out, they show me their constituent parts. There is something Romanian sitting inside many German words. In 'Frankfurt' there is 'theft', from the Romanian *furt*. And there is often something German sitting inside Romanian words, *pur* ['pure'] in *iepure*, the Romanian rabbit. Isn't it strange how many words are discreetly hiding inside other words? If I cut off the 't' at the end, *Landschaft* ['landscape'] becomes a *Landschaf* ['land sheep'], *Schirmherrschaft* ['patronage'] becomes a *Schirmherrschaf* ['patron sheep']. I always cut out the word *Jahrhunderte* ['centuries'] to have it in reserve, because it contains *Hunde* ['dogs'] with a lower-case first letter. I often need lower-case dogs, I can use them to make compound dogs: *Sommerhunde* ['summer dogs'] or *Heimwehhunde* ['homesickness dogs']. And *Herzkrankheit* ['heart disease'] contains a *Herzkran* ['heart crane'].

You notice all of this when you are cutting them out – with time, the words become constructions from which you can extract parts.

For what letters do you have a particularly large number of words?

When I look inside my drawers, it appears that there are words that love company and others that want to remain solitary. It depends on their first letters. With G, S, U, Z, the words are so common they fill the drawer, piled up at finger height. This suggests to me that they are cheeky and love a crowd. With other letters – H, I, L or P – my words are rarer, and it seems to me that they are shy, and that they prefer to be by themselves. This simply has to do with the number of words in the drawer, not with their meaning. The characteristics of a word sometimes even contradict its meaning. The word '*Herde*' ['herd'], for example, is more of a loner.

And when I need a word that I haven't yet cut out for a text, I have to stick it together out of the letters and syllables of other words. Sometimes, the act of cutting a word out has a long backstory. For example: '*pepita*' ['shepherd's check']. The word is rare, but it appears here and there in clothing catalogues. For years I didn't cut out the word '*pepita*', because in my first years in the city I had to wear an embarrassing pepita suit that had been sewn together by the village tailor. It even had silk-covered buttons. The trouser legs were too wide, and would flap round my feet. Even six, seven years later, my mother would still say how beautiful that pepita suit was. Besides, she would say, it's not like in the village: in the city you can wear anything; in the city no one knows you.

And then I found myself making a collage in which people were bathing in salad in a garden, with the words: 'when they came out they'd all eat a . . .'. And, well, the word '*pepita*' was ringing as a rhyme in my head: 'they'd all eat a pepita, particularly the ladies.' This was annoying. Now I needed the word! I started to search for it, leafing through one clothing catalogue after another, until my eyes were tired. Then I gave up, I had to stick the word together out of individual letters. It was exactly the same with the words *'Partei'* ['party'] and *'Diktator'* ['dictator']. For years, I never cut them out. I thought that they were dry, wooden terms that had nothing to do with my collages. But then things turned out differently. One day I needed them precisely because of their woodenness. Anyway, since then, I now always cut out *'pepita'*. Even if I already have the word ten times, I don't let it run away any more.

The emergencies, the contingencies, the congruencies are entirely different with cut-out words compared to ordinary writing. Even after more than twenty years of producing collages, they still astonish me. To this day, I still don't know what disposition is concealed within each word. This is only revealed when they come together in new ways.

This is also how I feel when I'm putting images together. The way in which their different elements combine is mysterious – and it needs to be mysterious. Sometimes the image reflects the text, sometimes it can't have anything to do with the text. My images are mostly built on fragments: parts of objects are combined with other parts of objects, and so a fictional object is created which surprises me. This is also how things started with the faces. I wanted to use a portrait for a collage, but to make the person in the photo unrecognisable. So I cut through the middle of a child's face. And what did I see? A child's face cut in half resembles an adult face in profile.

*The individual words you cut out are, in a
certain way, also images.*

The cut-out words are all different. Every word is another object, perhaps even an individual. Its appearance – the different sizes, the colours, the typeface – is just as import-ant for a collage as the meaning of the word. Essentially, it is the individuality of the words – which always look the same when you simply type them – which makes sticking them together so absorbing. Shall I use a yellow chessboard or a green one, a big word that will dominate the text or a small one that wants to hide? This cannot be predicted. It depends on the overall composition of the collage and on the words that I encounter.

There are also mysterious situations. For years I have always cut out '*doch*' ['but, yet'], but I have never yet cut out '*noch*' ['still, yet'], I can't explain this. Suddenly I need '*noch*' and I look inside my drawer and I don't have it. This makes me question my judgement. Why do I find '*noch*' so unremarkable that I have never cut it out?

I also have articles and prepositions in a huge variety of different typefaces and colours, of course: you always need them, whatever the sentences look like, and so I often have to juggle them. '*Das*' ['the'] I sometimes need written very big, in order to stretch out the line, while at other times I need it to be miniscule, in order to shorten the line, so that it will look good on the card when I glue it on.

I get this word hunger when I'm cutting words out – I am impatient – and then I keep cutting faster and faster, as if someone is going to steal the words off me if I don't cut them out fast enough.

How does each collage begin? Is it that, out of all the words, two suddenly shine out and you say: I'm going to do something with 'fox' and 'cloud' now?

Sometimes. Fox and cloud might get involved with each other, but there has to be a point to this interaction; the two nouns alone are not enough. And this is still only a starting point, just like with prose. Collages tell a story, too. And this starting point can slip into the middle, to the end, or it can be completely crowded out of the collage, as is the case with any piece of writing.

And on top of this comes the rhyme. But you shouldn't immediately see it in the collage; it shouldn't push itself to the front. Although it is the engine of the sentence, the sentences have to sound as if the rhyme has appeared of its own accord. I feel a great sense of intimacy with the rhyme, and want it to have its say. It can grieve, or wink, or it can make fun of the whole text. It determines the beat and the rhythm, because it binds lines together, and it carries the sound. It is like a watchman, but it is also a rascal; on the one hand it brings order to the collage, and on the other it catapults the text wherever it wants. It can be entirely unpredictable. It requires sentences of me that I had no inkling of beforehand, and I am often amazed by how long a short word can reverberate for after you have used it. It can echo in your head.

And then of course you have the image on top of this, too.

*So does the text determine the image or is it
the other way round?*

Usually the image is reacting to the text. I do often find myself making only images, though, and then a text will answer them afterwards. Either the image gets involved with the text, adding something to it, or it won't let itself be connected to the text thematically at all, and it stays standing alone beside it. Many of the stories make the image their own, while others want it to remain unclear whether they have anything to do with the image.

I can't usually tweak the text for the sake of an image. The text must fit entirely on the card. And due to the picture postcard format, space is scarce, so it can only fit on there as the shortest of stories anyway. It's always about concise storytelling. This is why the image always has to adapt to the length of the text. And if both of them can't fit on the card together, I have to make a smaller image for the collage in order to keep the text.

There are imageless days and there are textless days, days on which all attempts at images fail and others on which all texts fail. Then it's no use, you have to let go and wait for another day.

If one places the collage books next to each other, one sees how different they are, visually: in Im Haarknoten wohnt eine Dame [*In the Topknot Lives a Lady*]*, the colours are finely nuanced, the images are often larger than in the other books, and sometimes the text also runs into them. But the words in* Vater telefoniert mit den Fliegen [*Father's on the Phone with the Flies*] *are cut out so precisely; here we begin to see the master at work. And in* Die blassen Herren mit den Mokkatassen [*The Pale Gentlemen with their Espresso Cups*] *there are many blazing colours: a dazzling green, for example. Is this an accident, purely contingent on how these things were put together, or an artistic development?*

If only I knew. What I do know is that time passed between these pieces. Just like writing, the collages also change over time. For *Der Wächter nimmt seinen Kamm* [*The Guard Takes His Comb*], I started with a box. In the box, each collage was on an individual card. They were all black and white images, the words were all taken from newspapers and there were no rhymes. This was in the early 1990s. Today, every collage is like a relief, because before I cut any word out, I first stick two layers of cardboard beneath it. With two layers of cardboard underneath it, every word is as hard as a little plaque: there is a shadow border round it and the text lifts itself up from the cardboard. This is pleasing. Sometimes the empty card looks to me like a white handkerchief. And then the words settle on to it.

But you don't use newspaper words any more,
do you? You prefer to work with thicker,
shinier paper now?

Newspaper very quickly grows old. When I look inside a drawer, I can immediately see which words are made out of newspaper. Because I've had them for a long time, they are yellow. They also shrivel a little. I have two drawers full for every letter now, after all. I should probably throw over half of the words in one of my cabinets away, because they are these very small, old words. But I can't do it.

I also have a cabinet full of Romanian words.

In these three books there is only a single Romanian
line: 'The louse drinks blood in lilac / Ma cam
doare bila.'

Which means: 'my skull hurts'. This is informal language, and it's ironic: you wouldn't use '*bila*' to describe the head of someone with any brains: '*bila*' means 'noggin' in Romanian.

You only mix languages in exceptional cases;
you rarely slip in a foreign word.

That would then be an entirely different kind of text. But for two years I only made Romanian collages. I couldn't write in Romanian, and so I wanted to see whether I could make collages out of cut-out words from Romanian magazines. I could no longer get away from it: I could no longer get away from the language of the factory, from my friend Jenny's impertinent language, from the thirty-plus years I lived in Romania. Without realising, I ended up sticking together around two hundred Romanian collages. So now I have a Romanian collage book, and a whole cabinet full of Romanian words, which I will certainly never use again. I could throw them away now and make space for other words. But I find that I can't throw them away; they are at home here.

Does this way of writing – with a pair of scissors –
not also make these short texts more light-hearted?
Often, they involve a joke.

The themes of my collages are no different to those of my novels. Nevertheless, they have a certain lightness, because I have the feeling that it isn't me at all who is making the text with cut-out words – the words make it themselves.

I feel I am lucky to own hundreds of thousands of words. And when I am travelling, I often think of the fact that the words are waiting for me at home. The fact that they are allowed to lie around in the open is an expression of ease, of personal freedom. For my abundant ownership of words is the opposite of the past, the opposite of censorship. In the past, I had to carry what I had written away from my home in secret and hide it with acquaintances who would not arouse suspicion, because I was afraid of house searches.

Sometimes my cabinets with all these drawers seem to me like a train station, and I ask myself whether the words would like to set off for the text I'm working on, or would prefer to wait for some future, unforeseeable text. I also don't know whether they feel locked up inside the drawer, or whether they feel protected.

What most distinguishes the collages from my usual writing is that space is limited; the edge of the card is the end of the story. And once the words are stuck fast, you can't change anything. It's like life: something happens, and it can no longer be undone.

And the rhymes lay tracks, they are difficult to forget, they linger, repeating themselves of their own accord, because they have their own tempo and they echo in your head. And I walk on the asphalt and the echo won't leave me in peace and I know I have to catch the echo and say the rhyme to myself until the echo is empty and tired.

Walking and rhyming, I know that from the past. The rhyme that I would say to myself inside my own mouth as I was wandering around in those uncertain days would keep coming back to me again here, on the Berlin pavement, echoing the rhythm of my steps. I made it into a collage.

My fatherland was
an apple core, 'twixt
sickle and star we'd
pitch and yaw

And the image to go with it: a compound person. Thin long legs, standing on tiptoes, her chest a dark wooden box. And locked up inside the chest is her head.

Notes

Owls on the Roof

1   It creeps into us: 'Gelber Mais und keine Zeit'. In: *Immer derselbe Schnee und immer derselbe Onkel*, p. 128

4   to resemble the plants: 'In Every Language There Are Other Eyes'. In: *Cristina and Her Double*, p. 19

5   candidate[s] for the waxworks of death: 'In Every Language There Are Other Eyes'. In: *Cristina and Her Double*, p. 22

7   beautiful summer dresses: 'Nadirs'. In: *Nadirs*, p. 61

7   jewellery gleam: 'In Every Language There Are Other Eyes'. In: *Cristina and Her Double*, pp. 19–20

9   endure grief and learn to understand it: 'Denk nicht dorthin, wo du nicht sollst'. In: *Immer derselbe Schnee und immer derselbe Onkel*, p. 27

10   the other for the grass: 'Nadirs'. In: *Nadirs*, pp. 57–8

15   a hair clasp: 'When We Don't Speak We Become Unbearable – When We Do We Make Fools of Ourselves'. In: *Cristina and Her Double*, p. 171

15   key of heaven: 'Wenn etwas in der Luft liegt, ist es meist nichts Gutes'. In: *Der König verneigt sich und tötet*, p. 191

16   like army recruits: 'Wenn etwas in der Luft liegt, ist es meist nichts Gutes'. In: *Der König verneigt sich und tötet*, p. 194

16   leans its back against the fences: 'Niederungen'.
      In: *Niederungen*, p. 69 (passage not included in existing
      English translation)

16   pitch-black and dead silent: 'Nadirs'. In: *Nadirs*, p. 36

19   Do you have a handkerchief: 'Jedes Wort weiß etwas vom
      Teufelskreis'. In: *Immer derselbe Schnee und immer derselbe
      Onkel*, p. 7

22   nursery: 'Die rote Blume und der Stock'. In: *Der König
      verneigt sich und tötet*, p. 1157–8

The Rhyme Knows the Score

35   failing in public: 'Die Anwendung der dünnen Straßen'.
      In: *Immer derselbe Schnee und immer derselbe Onkel*,
      p. 118

47   beat and sound: 'When We Don't Speak We Become
      Unbearable – When We Do We Make Fools of Ourselves'.
      In: *Cristina and Her Double*, p. 173

52   in the snow: 'Niederungen'. In: *Niederungen*, p. 33 (passage
      not included in existing English translation)

The Clothes of Socialism

59   on the staircase: 'Jedes Wort weiß etwas vom Teufelskreis'.
      In: *Immer derselbe Schnee und immer derselbe Onkel*, p. 10

61   not in my nature: 'Jedes Wort weiß etwas vom
      Teufelskreis'. In: *Immer derselbe Schnee und immer derselbe
      Onkel*, p. 9

62   a witches' cauldron: 'Cristina and Her Double'.
      In: *Cristina and Her Double*, p. 59

68   clothes: *The Appointment*, p. 39

77   overflowing with cuckoo flower: 'When We Don't Speak
      We Become Unbearable – When We Do We Make Fools
      of Ourselves'. In: *Cristina and Her Double*, p. 182

78 get the better of chaos: 'In Every Language There Are Other Eyes'. In: *Cristina and Her Double*, p. 23

82 surprisingly beautiful: 'In Every Language There Are Other Eyes'. In: *Cristina and Her Double*, p. 32

85 grammar of feeling: 'Welt, Welt, Schwester Welt'. In: *Immer derselbe Schnee und immer derselbe Onkel*, p. 237

88 into their trumpets: 'Jedes Wort weiß etwas vom Teufelskreis'. In: *Immer derselbe Schnee und immer derselbe Onkel*, p. 17

A Man with a Bouquet

94 expelled from the Party: *The Land of Green Plums*, p. 25

99 didn't count any more: *The Land of Green Plums*, p. 29

103 exchanged fear for insanity: *The Land of Green Plums*, p. 41

104 dwarf lady with shaggy hair: 'Das Ticken der Norm'. In: *Hunger und Seide*, p. 94

106 deaf and unable to speak: *The Land of Green Plums*, p. 40

108 pant at love: *The Land of Green Plums*, p. 201

109 fly away together: *The Land of Green Plums*, p. 211

111 wandering: *The Land of Green Plums*, p. 38

114 planned fear: 'The King Bows Down and Kills'. In: *Cristina and Her Double*, p. 96. 'Die Anwendung der dünnen Straßen'. In: *Immer derselbe Schnee und immer derselbe Onkel*, p. 118

117 [love] grew claws: *The Land of Green Plums*, p. 76

120 Rolf Bossert: 'The King Bows Down and Kills'. In: *Cristina and Her Double*, p. 115

All Full of Cold Feelings

126 cut-up fox: *The Fox Was Ever the Hunter*, p. 158

135 kiss on the hand: *The Appointment*, p. 3

137 can't show that I'm learning: *The Appointment*, p. 22

138 eats a walnut: *The Appointment*, p. 15

139 tick on into the void: 'The King Bows Down and Kills'.
In: *Cristina and Her Double*, p. 99

140 it belongs to me: *The Appointment*, p. 203

141 dumb sense of satisfaction: 'The King Bows Down and
Kills'. In: *Cristina and Her Double*, p. 114

The Regime Buries Its Crimes

150 a female friend: *The Land of Green Plums*. 'Cristina and
Her Double' and 'When We Don't Speak We Become
Unbearable – When We Do We Make Fools of Ourselves'.
In: *Cristina and Her Double*.

157 your friend's visit and her confession: *The Appointment*,
p. 147 ff.

162 a tangle of love and betrayal: 'Cristina and Her Double'.
In: *Cristina and Her Double*, p. 71

163 frighteningly alive: 'When We Don't Speak We Become
Unbearable – When We Do We Make Fools of Ourselves'.
In: *Cristina and Her Double*, p. 176

165 hungry grasses: 'Einmal anfassen – zweimal loslassen'.
In: *Der König verneigt sich und tötet*, p. 103

165 victims of the secret service: 'Lügen haben kurze Beine –
die Wahrheit hat keine'. In: *Hunger und Seide*, p. 113

Two Sighs of Relief

168 didn't gain access to it: 'Cristina and Her Double'.
In: *Cristina and Her Double*, p. 55

175 write about it: 'Aber immer geschwiegen'. In: *Immer
derselbe Schnee und immer derselbe Onkel*, p. 171

180 merciful compeller: *The Hunger Angel*, p. 283

The Wonders of My Fatherland

184 comprehensible to them: 'Die Insel liegt innen – die Grenze liegt außen'. In: *Der König verneigt sich und tötet,* p. 175

184 foreign gaze: 'Der Fremde Blick'. In: *Der König verneigt sich und tötet,* p. 130

193 time standing still: *The Passport,* p. 7

198 a Securitate agent: *Traveling on One Leg,* p. 18

My Friend Oskar

206 where it came from: 'Die Anwendung der dünnen Straßen'. In: *Immer derselbe Schnee und immer derselbe Onkel,* p. 120

222 way home: *The Hunger Angel,* p. 188

224 the people from the camp: *The Hunger Angel,* p. 249

224 not pride: *The Hunger Angel,* p. 237

Drawers and Letters

229 aunt's tailoring workshop: 'Schneiderin'. In: *Die Nacht ist aus Tinte gemacht,* CD 1, 12

229 clothes for her dolls and cats: 'Nadirs'. In: *Nadirs,* p. 11

The following editions of works by Herta Müller are referred to in the present book

All the following works are in copyright. Extracts are reproduced by kind permission of the publishers.

Published in English translation

The Appointment (London: Granta, 2011), translated by Michael Hulse and Philip Boehm. Originally published in German as *Heute wär ich mir lieber nicht begegnet* (Reinbek bei Hamburg: Rowohlt Verlag, 2007).

Cristina and Her Double (London: Granta, 2013), translated by Geoffrey Mulligan. A collection of essays selected from the volumes in the original German: *Der König verneigt sich und tötet* [The King Bows Down and Kills] (Munich: Hanser Verlag, 2003), *Immer derselbe Schnee und immer derselbe Onkel* [Always the Same Snow and Always the Same Uncle] (Munich: Hanser Verlag, 2011), *Hunger und Seide* [Hunger and Silk] (Reinbek bei Hamburg: Rowohlt Verlag, 1995).

The Fox Was Ever the Hunter (London: Granta, 2017), translated by Philip Boehm. Originally published in German as *Der Fuchs war damals schon der Jäger* (Munich: Hanser Verlag, 2009).

The Hunger Angel (London: Granta, 2013), translated by Philip Boehm. Originally published in German as *Atemschaukel* (Munich: Hanser Verlag, 2009).

The Land of Green Plums (London: Granta, 1999), translated by

Michael Hofmann. Originally published in German as *Herztier* (Reinbek bei Hamburg: Rowohlt Verlag, 1994).

Nadirs (Lincoln: University of Nebraska Press, 1999). Originally published in German as *Niederungen* (Munich: Hanser Verlag, 2010).

The Passport (London: Serpent's Tail, 1989), translated by Martin Chalmers. Originally published in German as *Der Mensch ist ein großer Fasan auf der Welt* (Munich: Hanser Verlag, 2009).

Traveling on One Leg (Evanston: Northwestern University Press, 1998), translated by Valentina Glajar and André Lefevere. Originally published in German as *Reisende auf einem Bein* (Munich: Hanser Verlag, 2010).

Other titles

Die blassen Herren mit den Mokkatassen [The Pale Gentlemen with Their Espresso Cups] (Munich: Hanser Verlag, 2005).

Im Haarknoten wohnt eine Dame [In the Topknot Lives a Lady] (Reinbek bei Hamburg: Rowohlt Verlag, 2000).

Immer derselbe Schnee und immer derselbe Onkel [Always the Same Snow and Always the Same Uncle] (Munich: Hanser Verlag, 2011).

Der König verneigt sich und tötet [The King Bows Down and Kills] (Munich: Hanser Verlag, 2003).

Die Nacht ist aus Tinte gemacht: Herta Müller erzählt ihre Kindheit im Banat [The Night is Made of Ink: Herta Müller Talks About Her Childhood in Banat], two audio CDs (Wyk auf Föhr: supposé, 2009).

Der Wächter nimmt seinen Kamm. Vom Weggehen und Ausscheren [The Guard Takes His Comb. On Leaving and Changing Course] (Reinbek bei Hamburg: Rowohlt Verlag, 1993).

Vater telefoniert mit den Fliegen [Father's on the Phone with the Flies] (Munich: Hanser Verlag, 2012).